Toward Better Infrastructure

*Conditions, Constraints, and Opportunities
in Financing Public-Private Partnerships
in Select African Countries*

*Riham Shendy
Zachary Kaplan
Peter Mousley*

D0613379

THE WORLD BANK
Washington, D.C.

World Bank Studies are published to communicate the results of the Bank's work to the development community with the least possible delay. The manuscript of this paper therefore has not been prepared in accordance with the procedures appropriate to formally-edited texts. This volume is a product of the staff of the International Bank for Reconstruction and Development / The World Bank. The findings, interpretations, and conclusions expressed in this volume do not necessarily reflect the views of the Executive Directors of The World Bank or the governments they represent.

The World Bank does not guarantee the accuracy of the data included in this work. The boundaries, colors, denominations, and other information shown on any map in this work do not imply any judgement on the part of The World Bank concerning the legal status of any territory or the endorsement or acceptance of such boundaries.

ISBN: 978-0-8213-8781-8
eISBN: 978-0-8213-8820-4
DOI: 10.1596/978-0-8213-8781-8

Library of Congress Cataloging-in-Publication Data

Shendy, Riham.
 Towards better infrastructure : conditions, constraints, and opportunities in financing public-private partnerships : evidence from Cameroon, Côte d'Ivoire, Ghana, Kenya, Nigeria, and Senegal / Riham Shendy, Zachary Kaplan, Peter Mousley ; PPIAF.
    p. cm.
 "This report was produced at the request of the Government of Ghana (GOG) under the leadership of the Project Finance and Analysis (PFA) Unit of the Public Investment Department (PID) of the Ministry of Finance and Economic Planning (MOFEP) and with support from the World Bank and Public Private Infrastructure Advisory Facility (PPIAF)"--Acknowledgements.
 ISBN 978-0-8213-8781-8 -- ISBN 978-0-8213-8820-4
 1. Public-private sector cooperation--Africa. 2. Public works--Africa--Finance. 3. Infrastructure (Economics)--Africa. I. Kaplan, Zachary. II. Mousley, Peter. III. World Bank. IV. Public-Private Infrastructure Advisory Facility. V. Title.
 HD3872.A35S54 2011
 658.15224--dc22
                                                                                                    2011019769

Contents

Figures

Tables

Acknowledgments

This report was produced at the request of the Government of Ghana (GOG) under the leadership of the Project Finance and Analysis (PFA) Unit of the Public Investment Department (PID) of the Ministry of Finance and Economic Planning (MOFEP) and with support from the World Bank and Public Private Infrastructure Advisory Facility (PPIAF). The latter is a multidonor technical assistance facility aimed at helping developing countries improve the quality of their infrastructure through private sector involvement. The authoring team of Riham Shendy, Zachary Kaplan, and Peter Mousley would like to thank the MOFEP and the PFA Unit for their collaboration and guidance on this study. We would also offer our deep thanks to the Federal Government of Nigeria (FGN), specifically the Infrastructure Concession Regulatory Commission (ICRC), and the governments of Kenya, Senegal, Côte d' Ivoire, and Cameroon. Input for this report for the Francophone countries was made possible by the background report completed by Axelcium Consultants and for the Anglophone countries from Benjamin Darche and Thomas Cochran. We extend our thanks to our colleagues at PPIAF who provided the resources for this study. World Bank staff who have also provided guidance and feedback include Clemente Del Valle, Sophie Sirtaine, Jordan Schwartz, Subrahmanya Pulle Srinivas, Sri Kumar Tadimalla, Clive Harris, Jeffery Demon, Iain Menzies, and Dante Reyes. Vivien Foster and Cecelia M. Briceño-Garmendia were instrumental for their work on the Africa Infrastructure Country Diagnostics (AICD) Report and for providing generous advice on the infrastructure data. We also thank private sector entities for their input at various stages of drafting this report: Ecobank in Ghana, Stanbic Bank in Nigeria, and Macquarie Group in South Africa, the latter during the PPP forum in the 2010 Spring Meeting. Additional thanks to Robert Holzman for his valuable input on the potential role of pensions in infrastructure financing and to Varsha Marathe and Tatiana Nenova for their guidance, respectively, on the India and Bangladeshi financial intermediary loan arrangements for PPP financing.

A workshop presenting the financing section of this study took place in Accra on December 6, 2010. The event was chaired by the National Development Planning Commission Chairman Mr P. V. Obeng, together with the World Bank Country Director, Ishac Diwan. The workshop was attended by a wide number of stakeholders: MoFEP, Bank of Ghana , National Insurance Commission (NIC), Social Security and National Insurance Trust (SSNIT), the Ministry of Roads and Highways, Ministry of Transport, Ministry of Energy, Ghana Stock Exchange, and Ghana Ports and Harbor Authority. In addition, representatives from the private sector included: African Finance Corporation, AB & David Law Firm, National Investment Bank, Barclays Bank, PriceWaterhouseCoopers, Standard Chartered Bank, and the Financial Times. The African Development Bank and the World Bank Group (with representatives from IFC and MIGA) also participated. We thank all participants for their useful feedback.

Finally, the authors would like to note that the focus of this report is to scope out and describe in an introductory fashion the factors affecting long-term financing for public-private partnerships (PPPs) in the sample countries. The report further describes the current PPP initiatives in Cameroon, Côte D'Ivoire, Ghana, Kenya, Nigeria, and Senegal and highlights the general challenges regarding the enabling environment required for PPP programs. Noting that "one size does not fit all" and that addressing financial and capital market constraints and designing a PPP program may vary significantly across countries, this analysis is meant to lay the groundwork for more in-depth country-specific diagnostics that will explore and expand on the concepts touched upon in this study. Indeed, each section merits its own analytical review. Furthermore we highlight that segments of this report outline other country PPP experiences, such as the pension market in Peru and changes in banking prudential norms in India. The authors note that in some instances the reforms are so recent that it is too early to draw conclusions on their effectiveness; they are therefore used in this report illustratively rather than as specific recommendations to be pursued.

Acronyms and Abbreviations

AICD	Africa Infrastructure Country Diagnostics
APIX	Agence Nationale chargée de la Promotion de l'Investissement des Grands Travaux
BIDC	Banque D'Investissement et de Développement de la Cedeao, also EBID
BOAD	West African Development Bank
BOT	Build/Operate/Transfer
BRVM	Bourse Régionale des Valeur Mobiliers
CAD Fund	China-Africa Development Fund
CEPIP	Ministry of Economic Infrastructure and the Investment Promotion Center
CET	Construction-Exploitation-Transfert (French equivalent of BOT)
CIC	China Investment Corporation
CIMA	Inter-African Conference for the Insurance Market
CMA	Capital Market Authority
DASP	La Direction de l'Appui au Secteur Privé
DSX	Douala Stock Exchange
EAIF	Emerging Africa Infrastructure Fund
EBID	ECOWAS Bank for Investment and Development , also BIDC
ECOWAS	The Economic Community of West African States
EOI	Expression of Interest
FANAF	La Fédération des Sociétés d'Assurances de Droit National Africaines
FGN	Federal Government of Nigeria
FSAP	Financial Sector Assessment Program
GOG	Government of Ghana
GSE	Ghana Stock Exchange
ICRC	Infrastructure Concession Regulatory Commission
IFC	International Finance Corporation
IGF	Indonesia Infrastructure Guarantee Fund
IFI	International Financial Institutions
IFS	International Financial Statistics
IMF	International Monetary Fund
IPP	Independent Power Plant
MDA	Ministry, Department and Agency
MoF	Ministry of Finance
MOFEP	Ministry of Finance and Economic Planning
NGN	Nigerian Naira
NIC	National Insurance Commission
NSE	Nairobi Stock Exchange

NSE	Nigeria Stock Exchange
PAU	Project Advisory Unit
PFA	Project Finance and Analysis Unit
PIDG	Private Infrastructure Development Group
PPI	Private Participation in Infrastructure
PPIAF	Public-Private Infrastructure Advisory Facility
PPP	Public-Private Partnership
PCG	Partial Credit Guarantee
PRG	Partial Risk Guarantee
RBA	Retirement Benefit Authority
REC	Regional Economic Communities
SME	Small and Medium Enterprise
SPV	Special Purpose Vehicle
SSA	Sub-Saharan Africa
SSNIT	Social Security and National Insurance Trust
SWF	Sovereign Wealth Funds
TMRC	Tanzania Mortgage Refinance Corporation
VfM	Value for Money
VGF	Viability Gap Fund/ Facility
WAMEU	West Africa Monetary and Economic Union
WDI	World Development Indicators
WEO	World Economic Output

Overview

Examining innovative ways to address Africa's infrastructure deficit is at the heart of this analysis. Africa's infrastructure stock and quality is among the least developed in the world, a challenge that significantly hinders economic development. It is estimated that the finance required to raise infrastructure in Sub Saharan Africa (SSA) to a reasonable level within the next decade is at US$93 billion per year, with two-thirds of this amount needed for capital expenditures. With the existing spending on infrastructure being estimated at US$45 billion per annum and after accounting for potential efficiency gains that could amount to US$17 billion, Africa's infrastructure funding gap remains around US$31 billion a year. One approach to address this challenge is by facilitating the increase of private provision of public infrastructure services through public-private partnerships (PPPs). This approach, which is a relatively new arrangement in SSA is multifaceted and requires strong consensus and collaboration across both public and private sectors.

There are several defined models of PPPs. Each type differs in terms of government participation levels, risk allocations, investment responsibilities, operational requirements, and incentives for operators. Our definition of PPPs assumes transactions where the private sector retains a considerable portion of commercial and financial risks associated with a project. In more descriptive terms, among the elements defining the notion of PPPs discussed in this study are: a long-term contract between a public and private sector party; the design, construction, financing, and operation of public infrastructure by the private sector; payment over the life of the PPP contract to the private sector party for the services delivered from the asset; and the facility remaining in public ownership or reverting to public sector ownership at the end of the PPP contract. The observations and policy recommendations that follow draw on ongoing World Bank Group PPP engagements in these countries, including extensive consultations with key public and private sector stakeholders involved in designing, financing, and implementing PPPs.

The study is structured around the most inhibiting constraints to developing PPPs, as shared by all six countries. Section 1 provides a brief background of the infrastructure needs in the sample countries and outlines the current scope of PPP transactions; Section 2 examines the sources of financing for PPPs—domestic and foreign—with a particular focus on domestic sources; Section 3 explores the supporting legislative, regulatory, and institutional environment for PPPs; Section 4 addresses issues connected with the importance of developing a sound pipeline of PPP projects; and Section 5 tackles the importance of managing the increased government fiscal commitments that are commonly coupled with PPPs. Section 6 outlines medium-term options for PPP financing. Finally, Section 7 puts forth policy recommendations intended to assist in overcoming the challenges in building private sector confidence in the SSA infrastructure market in order to attract greater levels of financing for private sector investment in core infrastructure services through PPPs.

Main Findings

The constraints that the private sector faces in accessing the core infrastructure market in the six targeted countries can be divided into two broad categories: financial limitations and a weak PPP enabling environment. Primary *financial limitations* include access to local currency and affordable long-term debt and the need for government support to the capital investment required to make a PPP transaction commercially viable. The *weak PPP enabling environment* calls for a clearer legal and regulatory framework; improved competitive bidding procedures; more consistent sector policies, including tariff regimes that allow for greater, if not complete cost recovery; a more robust PPP pipeline; and strengthened management of fiscal commitments from PPPs.

Financial constraints…

There is an overall shortage of long-term locally denominated debt financing. Examining potential sources for PPP financing in the financial and capital markets suggests the underdeveloped financing environment in the six selected countries. The size of local commercial banks is small relative to the significant funding required for infrastructure projects; loans have short tenors, with a maximum of five years; there are no long-term pricing benchmarks because of a short government yield curve; and banks lack the experience and skill to undertake project financing. Regarding institutional investors, while the life insurance market is small for the Anglophone sample countries, public pensions can potentially be a source of PPP financing. However a significant level of capital market development is needed before such funds can be used.

International sources of financing for PPPs do offer some alternatives to local domestic sources but cannot replace a strong local financial and capital market. International commercial banks are to some extent involved in infrastructure investments, and most have been operating under the umbrella of a donor or an export credit agency to minimize loans' political and commercial risk. Private infrastructure funds have mostly invested in telecommunications; however they have dried up as a result of the recent financial crisis. The latter, coupled with the high risks for most PPP transactions in SSA, deter a good deal of international financing. While donor-supported infrastructure funds (and sovereign wealth funds to a small degree) are strategic and catalytic for the PPP financing market, they are still limited in scope and size in light of the demand for infrastructure in SSA.

… and a poor enabling environment

Legislation and policies governing PPPs remain unclear, inconsistent and inhibit private sector investors from participating in the infrastructure market. Private investors are hesitant because of a general lack of competitive and transparent bidding processes, undefined or unknown tariff regimes, and inconsistent strategies for engaging with the private sector across the different sectors/industries. This often results in signaling a weak or uncertain government commitment to a PPP transaction.

Unclear institutional arrangements on how a PPP transaction is developed, vetted, and implemented, additionally conflicting agendas across government agencies stall transactions from developing in a timely, efficient, and consistent fashion. Private sector investors are comforted by clear methods of interacting with the key public sector entities and simplified processing steps. Confusing government arrangements, inharmonious approaches among sponsoring government agencies, and opaque roles and responsibilities deter private sector involvement.

The currently limited financing available for PPPs can also be attributed to the lack of a good supply of PPP transactions developed with upstream analysis and other project-related due diligence that can credibly demonstrate the commercial potential for private sector investment. Many consultations with investors emphasized the inability for governments to demonstrate commercially viable deal flow of projects as the single most challenging part of the investment process. Private sector investors are interested in well-developed PPP transactions sponsored by governments that have performed upstream prefeasibility analysis to determine the best path toward private sector engagement and show solid government commitment to implementing the transaction alongside the private sector. A key issue related to transaction design is ensuring cost recovery for a proposed investment in a PPP project, either through reformed sector tariff policies that allow for tariff adjustment mechanisms, or alternatively through government support in the form of availability payments or revenue guarantees.

PPPs are commonly associated with fiscal liabilities, which if not well managed can potentially erode the perceived advantages of PPPs. There is a range of risks associated with PPP projects: political risks (made more difficult given elections and the uncertainty this can create in respect of policy changes), construction risk, financing risks, and so forth. It is critical to mitigate these risks and provide assurance to the private sector that policy focus will not be lost regardless of the political cycles taking place in the country of business. This is most sustainably done by creating a strong policy, legal and institutional foundation. Additionally a government must strengthen its expertise to carry out proper risk assessment on projects (including Value for Money-VfM analysis to determine if a PPP arrangement is best suited) and manage any fiscal liabilities that may be associated a PPP transaction. Together, these factors will reduce the riskiness of a project and help crowd in private investment.

Recommendations

As previously noted, in a number of stakeholder consultations undertaken in preparation of this report, the absence of a robust and bankable pipeline of PPP projects is highlighted as a primary concern. Addressing this entails a range of reforms and institutional developmental actions to mobilize deeper financing markets for PPPs. It includes: (i) building a clear and transparent PPP policy, legislative, regulatory (particularly regarding procurement), and institutional framework; (ii) defining clear roles and responsibilities across the central and sector-line ministries, departments, and agencies (MDAs) and their subsidiary government entities, to smooth the implementation of PPP projects, including the capacity building of MDAs to fulfill these mandates; (iii) providing budgetary support to produce a quality pipeline of PPP projects that employ upstream feasibility analysis to review projects properly and outline government contributions deemed necessary to make them commercially viable; (iv) fostering project finance capabilities within key institutions in the financial sector; (v) initiating the PPP program with carefully identified pilot PPP projects to showcase a successful transaction; (vi) managing effectively fiscal liabilities related to PPPs; and (vii) developing and implementing an effective communications strategy to government and private sector stakeholders and citizens to set out the steps—legal, policy, operational, and environmental and social safeguards—that the government will take to establish itself as a credible PPP "market maker" and a reliable partner to private investors and an accountable enabler of better service delivery to the population.

Within this broader PPP market-building context, the development of a specific market for long-term local financing can become more sustainable. Governments can develop the long-term local financing for infrastructure by supporting structural reforms; this includes developing the local capital market: the government and nongovernment bond markets; the equity and hybrid equity markets; and existing constraints in legislation and regulations that impede investor recourse to these markets when seeking to finance a PPP. Further development of the pension and insurance industry to facilitate institutional investment in infrastructure assets should also be pursued while recognizing this requires attainment of a certain track record of PPP performance to address the conservative risk tolerance of pension and insurance fund managers. However, to help close key financing gaps and promote private investment over the medium term, as these longer-gestating capital market changes take effect, governments can provide private project sponsors with commercial long-term finance by on-lending through various apex financial intermediaries, including Central Bank-administered funds, development banks, and specialized infrastructure financing facilities. Governments can obtain support from International Financial Institutions (IFIs) to establish such apex intermediaries and to adequately price the loan tenors to be provided.

The public sector should provide tools that enhance private sector engagement such as risk mitigation products and financial incentives. This includes: (i) supporting PPP projects with a Viability Gap Facility (VGF) to reduce the entrance cost for the private sector and make infrastructure assets more commercially viable; (ii) developing intermediate pricing strategies that contribute to the lengthening of the yield curve in ways that build the long-term debt market; (iii) providing mitigation products for political risk; and (iv) developing the PPP roles of Regional Economic Communities (RECs) and regionally active financial institutions to address the additional market failures that can impact smaller economies and regional and cross-border infrastructure needs.

Finally, it is important to manage government expectations regarding what one can expect from private participation in infrastructure, with respect to the size of their contribution and also the time required for processing PPP projects. While the private sector can significantly contribute to public services provision, the bulk of infrastructure will remain a government responsibility. It is worthwhile to note that PPP projects in the UK under the Private Finance Initiative (PFI) make up 10-15 percent of public's sector investment, and account for 20 and 15 percent of infrastructure investment in Spain and teh Republic of Korea, respectively. This indicates a benchmark in countries where PPPs have been active for at least a decade. Additionally and in light of the complexity of designing PPPs, they require lead time which can be longer than those needed under public procurement. For instance in the UK average time needed to reach financial close has varied from 18 months for the roads sector to 40 months for the health sector.

CHAPTER 1

Background

Current Status of PPP Markets in Selected Countries

The infrastructure deficit estimated for sub-Saharan Africa (SSA) is substantially high-er than what domestic resources can meet.[1] The finance required to raise infrastructure in SSA to a reasonable level within the next decade is estimated at US$93 billion per year, about 15 percent of regional GDP. This estimate covers the Information and Communications Technology (ICT), irrigation, power, transport, and water supply and sanitation sectors. Two-thirds of this amount is needed for capital expenditures and one-third to operate and maintain the infrastructure assets. Of the total required amount, the existing spending on infrastructure is estimated at US$45 billion per annum, of which around US$30 billion is financed by the African taxpayers and infrastructure users and US$15 billion is from external sources. After accounting for potential efficiency gains that could amount to US$17 billion, Africa's infrastructure funding gap still remains around US$31 billion a year. While the infrastructure needs for each of the SSA countries varies greatly, there is little doubt that the general shortfall in infrastructure services hampers economic growth by hindering productivity, increasing the costs of doing business, and isolating markets. Public sources continue to finance the majority of these investments, but governments across the continent are increasingly realizing that these resources are insufficient to finance the level of investment required to close the infrastructure deficit.

Annual public expenditures on infrastructure pale in comparison with the amounts required.[2] Figure 1.1 shows that most governments in SSA spend about 6-12 percent of their GDP each year on infrastructure, comprising the ICT, power, roads, and water and sanitation sectors. Approximately half of the countries spend more than 8 percent of GDP while a quarter of countries spend less than 5 percent (a level in line with Organiza-tion for Economic Co-operation and Development, OECD, counties). As indicated in the figure, most countries in the region spend less than US$600 million a year on infrastruc-ture services or equivalently less than US$50 per person. While these fiscal commitments seem large when expressed as a share of GDP compared to the actual nominal invest-ment values, they are small when placed in the context of the amounts needed.

Infrastructure data from the AICD reports for the countries under study highlight existing inefficiencies and infrastructure funding gaps. Figures 1.2 and 1.3 compile in-formation from the AICD country reports for Côte d'Ivoire, Ghana, Kenya, Nigeria, and Senegal.[3] Figure 1.2 displays the size of additional resources that could be recovered each year by improving efficiency. Provided that these inefficiencies could be fully ad-dressed, figure 1.3 shows the annual funding gap that needs to be met over the next 10 years to improve basic infrastructure to the level of a middle-income country such as

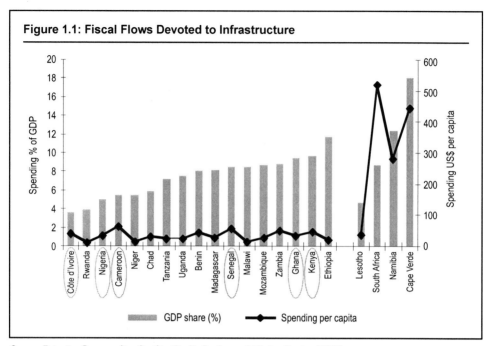

Source: Briceño-Garmendia, Cecilia, Karlis Smits, and Vivien Foster (2008).

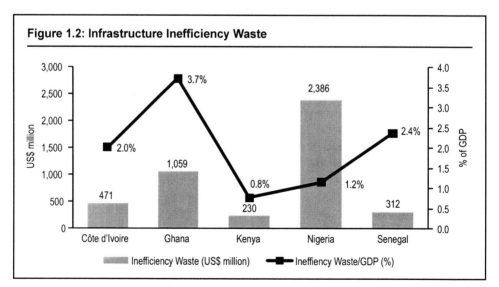

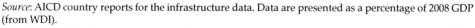

Source: AICD country reports for the infrastructure data. Data are presented as a percentage of 2008 GDP (from WDI).
Note: Ghana GDP figures incorporate the revisions undertaken by the GoG in November 2010.

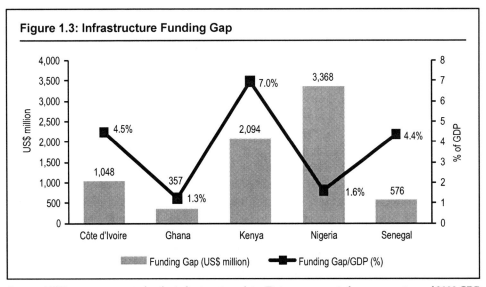

Figure 1.3: Infrastructure Funding Gap

Source: AICD country reports for the infrastructure data. Data are presented as a percentage of 2008 GDP (from WDI).
Note: Ghana GDP figures incorporate the revisions undertaken by the GoG in November 2010.

Mauritius. While Kenya exhibits the lowest levels of infrastructure inefficiency waste, totaling US$230 million per annum (0.8 percent of GDP), the country's funding gap is the highest among all five countries marking US$2,094 million (7.0 percent of GDP). Contrarily, Ghana which exhibits the highest waste of resources estimated at US$1,059 million (3.7 percent of GDP), has the lowest levels of funding gap at US$357 million per annum (1.3 percent of GDP).

Leveraging private sector financing through PPPs is one option that is increasingly being pursued to help address the infrastructure gap. Arguably private sector participation in infrastructure can bring experience, efficiency, and finance in providing quality infrastructure services at better value for money than traditional government procurement. Numerous instances where the public and private sectors have joined to address a key infrastructure constraint have proved successful for all parties involved—the public sector is able to transfer risks to the private sector and reduce the overall amount of public funds necessary to complete the project, while the private sector accesses a commercial market with the potential for attractive financial returns. Examples of successful PPPs, such as telecom investments in SSA or toll roads in South Africa, hold the promise that PPPs can assume a significant role in solving Africa's infrastructure deficit. However it should be noted that providing the bulk infrastructure will remain a government responsibility. PPP projects in the UK under the Private Finance Initiative (PFI) make up 10-15 percent of public's sector investment, and account for 20 percent and 15 percent of Spain's and Korea's infrastructure investment respectively.[4] Notably, while PPPs can in fact be instrumental in accelerating development, they also present a new set of challenges for the public sector. For example, bringing the private sector in as investors and operators requires governments to adjust and implement policies to enable a systematic, consistent, coherent, and effective framework for private sector entry, operation, and exit from the PPP market.

While the literature comparing the efficiency of the public versus the private sector is limited for developing countries, several studies have documented the prominent role of private participation in a number of cross-country studies and in developed economies. The World Bank (2005, 2006, 2009), based on 14 case studies from rail concessions in SSA since the early 1990s, highlight that rail concessions have suffered if measured by returns to private sector investments and revenue collection; nevertheless results have been promising from a productivity perspective—productive efficiency has improved and labor productivity has increased steadily in all concession operating for over five years, and allocative efficiency appears to be increasing.[5] Gassner and Pushak (2008) examine the impact of private sector participation in water and electricity distribution using a data set of more than 1,200 utilities in 71 developing and transition economies. The results of the study show that the private sector delivers on expectations of higher labor productivity and operational efficiency, convincingly outperforming a set of comparable companies that remained state owned and operated. These findings echo those for Latin American countries where Andres (2004) and Andres, Foster, and Guasch (2006) find significant increases in quality, investment, and labor productivity and a decrease in employment in telecommunications, electricity, and water distribution services.

For developed countries there is ample evidence on the efficiency role of the private sector. Arthur Andersen & LSE (2000) evaluated 29 projects in the UK already in operation, a third of all PPPs in the UK at that time, showed that the average percentage estimated saving (against a public sector comparator) was 17 percent. Risk transfer accounted for 60 percent of forecast cost savings. Additionally the National Audit Office in the UK in 2003 examined construction performance in 37 UK projects compared to projects built by the public sector. The results show: 80 percent of PPP/PFI deals delivered price certainty; small price increases were evident in 20 percent of deals; 73 percent of publicly built projects experienced significant cost overruns; 66 percent of PPP deals delivered on time compared to 30 percent for those publicly built. Furthermore, in Finland the motorway between Helsinki and Lahti was built five years earlier than expected through a PPP and at lower cost.[6] Finally, figures published by the European Construction Industry Federation (FIEC) in December 2010 state that the global saving of PPPs is estimated around 25 percent compared to classical procurement[7]. This evidence on sound performances of private participation should not been regarded in isolation of the critical role attributed to the correct enabling environment being in place.

The data emphasizes the currently limited role of private participation in infrastructure (PPI) in the countries in this study. Figures 1.4 to 1.7 display the size of PPI in the six sample countries by both sector and PPP type; figures 1.5 and 1.7 exclude the telecom sector. Figure 1.4 shows that Nigeria and Ghana have attracted the largest PPIs as a percentage of GDP, 21 percent. It is worth mentioning that most of these deals are in the telecom subsector. Excluding the telecom industry and examining sectors that have a long-term cost recovery horizon and a more difficult risk profile, PPI as a percentage of GDP ranges from a low of 1 percent in Côte d'Ivoire to a high of 6 percent in Senegal (figure 1.5). These figures compare with Chile, India, and South Africa, where PPIs in

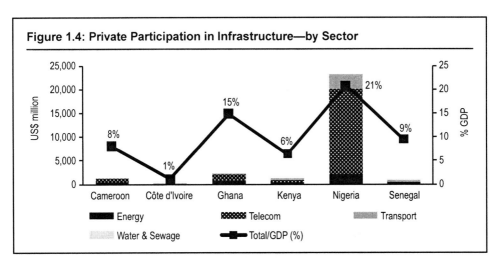

Figure 1.4: Private Participation in Infrastructure—by Sector

Source: World Bank and PPIAF (PPI Database covering 2000-09), GDP data: Average GDP between 2000 and 2009, from WDI.

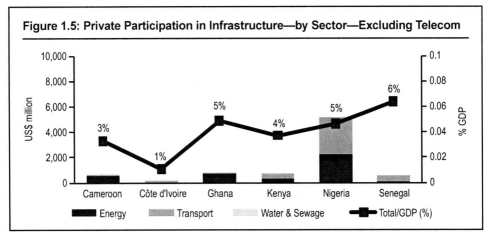

Figure 1.5: Private Participation in Infrastructure—by Sector—Excluding Telecom

Source: World Bank and PPIAF (PPI Database covering 2000-09), GDP data: Average GDP between 2000 and 2009, from WDI.

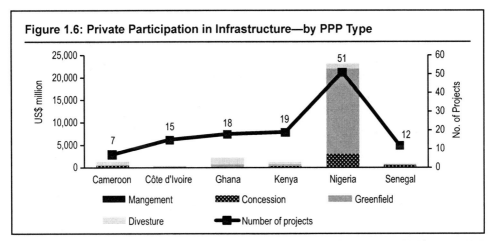

Figure 1.6: Private Participation in Infrastructure—by PPP Type

Source: World Bank and PPIAF (PPI Database covering 2000-09), GDP data: Average GDP between 2000 and 2009, from WDI.

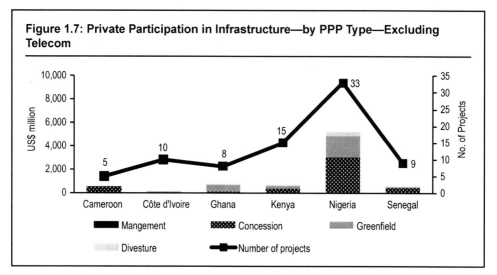

Figure 1.7: Private Participation in Infrastructure—by PPP Type—Excluding Telecom

Source: World Bank and PPIAF (PPI Database covering 2000-09), GDP data: Average GDP between 2000 and 2009, from WDI.

the non-telecom subsector accounted for 8 percent, 10 percent, and 3 percent of GDP, respectively. With respect to the type of PPP across all four sectors, together Greenfield and concession projects accounted for a low of 35 percent of the total value of the deals in Ghana to a high of 100 percent of the deals in Senegal. Excluding the telecom sector, these figures read a low of 76 percent for Côte d'Ivoire and high of 100 percent for all Cameroon, Ghana, and Senegal.

This Report

This analysis addresses the conditions, opportunities, and constraints in financing a PPP market in our sample countries based on a definition of PPPs that entails risk sharing between government and private parties in the provision of public services. There are several defined models of PPPs. Each type differs in terms of government participation levels, risk allocations, investment responsibilities, operational requirements, and incentives for operators. Our definition of PPPs assumes transactions where the private sector retains a considerable portion of commercial and financial risks associated with a project.[8] In more descriptive terms, among the elements defining the notion of PPPs discussed in this study are: a long-term contract between a public and private sector party; the design, construction, financing, and operation of public infrastructure by the private sector; payment over the life of the PPP contract to the private sector party for the use of the asset (such payments can be by either the public sector party or user fees); and the facility remaining in public ownership or reverting to public sector ownership at the end of the PPP contract.[9] As will be emphasized in the report, the public sector role in this partnership is critical in supporting an enabling environment for PPPs that would boost private investors' confidence. Additionally, governments need to endorse the premise of the PPP financial model that is based on cost recovery that ensures the commerciality of PPP projects, which can be achieved through undertaking sector tariff policy reforms or through government subsidies.

Support for PPPs rests on two principal propositions, flexible financing, and efficiency gains. The first proposition is that, through the involvement of private sector investment, public financing requirements for infrastructure can be spread over a longer time horizon leading—in any given fiscal space—to a faster expansion of infrastructure service provision. The second advantage rests on the efficiency gains argument associated with PPI. With PPPs, the current government saves in investment outlays; however, it either relinquishes future user fee revenue (in the case that the PPP is financed with user fees) or future tax revenues (if the PPP is anyway financed with payments from the government budget).[10] In this respect, the efficiency gains achieved through bundling the financing, design, construction, operation, and maintenance of infrastructure is the key cost-saving element in the PPP, rather than involvement of private finance per se.

Feedback from the private sector on the main determinants of demand for investing in PPP projects in SSA countries revealed a common set of weaknesses. Private partners, being concessionaires, investors, or financiers, highlight a number of obstacles to undertaking PPPs in SSA that can be grouped into three components. First, obtaining private financing for infrastructure projects can be a challenge in countries with underdeveloped financial and capital markets. Second, most counties lack a clear legislative and policy environment in which PPP projects can be developed, inclusive of sector-specific policies. Third, while there is no shortage of infrastructure projects in these countries envisaged as PPPs, very few if any have undergone proper upstream due diligence and analysis to determine their commercial viability and potential risk allocation scenarios.

This report is composed of six chapters. Addressing the determinants of demand from the private sector to invest in PPP projects calls for a comprehensive look at the enabling environment in the countries. In this report four sets of issues are seen to contribute to a conducive environment for PPPs. The first issue (discussed in Chapter 2) examines both the sources of financing for PPPs with a particular focus on domestic sources while also outlining foreign sources of finance. Issue two (Chapter 3) explores the supporting legislative, regulatory, and institutional environment. Issue three (Chapter 4) addresses the importance of developing a sound pipeline of PPP projects. Issue four (Chapter 5) tackles the concern of increased government fiscal commitments that are likely to arise from undertaking PPPs. Chapter 6 outlines some actions that can be considered over the medium term to assist in overcoming financing constraints to private sector involvement confidence in the sub-Saharan infrastructure market. Finally, Chapter 7 outlines the report policy recommendations.

Notes

1. Foster, Vivien, and Cecilia Briceño-Garmendia (2010).
2. Briceño-Garmendia, Cecilia, Karlis Smits, and Vivien Foster (2008).
3. There is no AICD report for Cameroon.
4. Yescombe (2007).
5. This information is based on Richard Bullock (2005; 2009) and Borgo (2006). A primary caveat to these studies as noted by the authors is that only two rail concessions have been in operation for more than five years (in part because of the government's poor ability to engage the private sector properly with a well-formed concession strategy)
6. All citations in the paragraph are from Sein (2006).
7. Infrastructure Investor (January 2011).

8. Guasch (2004) defines 12 arrangements, ordered by increasing private participation: public supply and operation, outsourcing, corporatization and performance agreement, management contracts, leasing (affermage), franchise, concession, build-operate-transfer (BOT), build-own-operate (BOO), divestiture by license, divestiture by sale, and private supply and operation. Our definition of PPP includes the four categories grouped by Guasch as concessions, namely, leasing, franchise, concession, and BOT.
9. Yescombe (2007).
10. EIB Papers (2010).

CHAPTER 2

Sources of Financing

Changes in sources of finance over the PPP project life cycle are determined by the different incentive problems associated with the construction and operational phases. The EIB (2010) report provides an overview of the structure of the financing cycle of PPP projects (figure 2.1). During construction, expenses are commonly financed with sponsor equity (which may be complemented with bridge loans and subordinated or mezzanine debt) and bank loans. This is because the construction phase is subject to substantial uncertainty, where major changes to the specifications of the project can occur, leaving ample room for moral hazard. In this respect banks are best suited to provide the debt component of the financing package during construction and to mitigate moral hazard by exercising tight control over changes to the project's contract and the behavior of the Special Purpose Vehicle (SPV)[1] and its contractors (Construction and O&M contractors). This control is achieved as banks disburse funds only gradually when project stages are

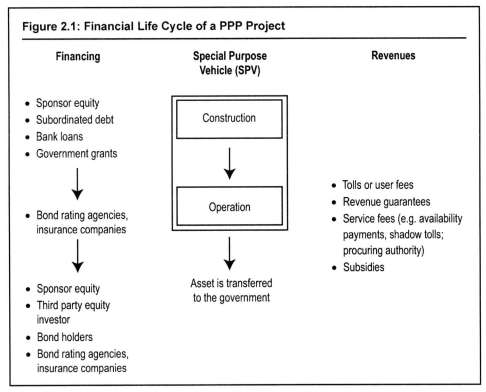

Figure 2.1: Financial Life Cycle of a PPP Project

Financing	Special Purpose Vehicle (SPV)	Revenues

- Sponsor equity
- Subordinated debt
- Bank loans
- Government grants

Construction

↓

- Bond rating agencies, insurance companies

Operation

- Tolls or user fees
- Revenue guarantees
- Service fees (e.g. availability payments, shadow tolls; procuring authority)
- Subsidies

- Sponsor equity
- Third party equity investor
- Bond holders
- Bond rating agencies, insurance companies

Asset is transferred to the government

Source: EIB (2010).

completed. As the PPP project becomes operational and the risks become more limited to events that may affect cash flows, long-term bonds substitute for bank loans, and the sponsor often seeks to be bought out by a facilities operator, or even by third-party passive investors, usually institutional investors. Notably bond finance is associated with two additional entities, rating agencies and insurance companies, which have critical roles to play in the issuance of bonds. The credit rating agency issues a rating of the SPV and with this rating the SPV buys insurance that increases the rating of the bond to investment grade or higher, thus enabling the selling of these bonds to institutional and other investors.

Sources of Local Financing for PPP Projects

There are overarching factors that limit Africa's ability to draw on long-term local and foreign currency financing for infrastructure.[2] *First,* most African countries have low or sometimes nonexistent sovereign credit ratings. Table 2.1 shows that our sample countries all exhibit noninvestment-grade foreign currency long-term sovereign debt ratings.[3] The low or nonexistent credit rating limits the public sector's ability to use private investors. *Second,* most local financial markets have limited capacity to finance infrastructure projects. PPP projects are high risk; local long-term resource markets are shallow; and infrastructure projects have required substantial credit enhancement provided mostly by official agencies to attract long term debt. *Third,* PPP projects tend to have longer payback and build-out periods and are more susceptible to political and regulatory interference. In light of these constraints the PPP projects implemented in SSA to date have typically been small relative to those in other regions. Many have been financed entirely with equity. Projects with faster payback, shorter-term debt, and limited regulatory intervention (such as telecommunications) and projects with US dollar revenue (such as export-oriented ports and railways, and gas pipelines) have been favored over projects with domestic revenues flows that require long-term financing to provide services at affordable prices over long payback periods (such as toll roads).

Table 2.1: Country Statistics

	Cameroon	Côte d'Ivoire	Ghana	Kenya	Nigeria	Senegal
Population (in millions 2009)	19.93	21.39	23.11	35.88	151.87	12.82
GDP per Capita ($ 2009)	1,136	1,105	1,097	738	1,118	1,023
Long-Term Foreign Currency Sovereign Debt Rating:						
S&P	B	N/A	B	B+	B+	B+
Fitch	B	N/A	B+	B+	BB-	N/A

Source: For Population and GDP per Capita figures: WEO-IMF Database March 2010 and WDI (Jan 2011), respectively. For *Sovereign* Rating: Bloomberg December 2010.

While mobilizing foreign financing for private infrastructure is important, a number of factors highlight that it is critical to develop a local market for PPPs. A primary factor demonstrated during the recent financial crisis is the volatility of international fina*nce.* Based on the World Economic Output (WEO) Report (April 2010), it is estimated that foreign banks decreased their total loan exposure to SSA by around 15 percent (US$14.4 billion) during the period from September 2008 to June 2009. Notably, almost half the withdrawal of funds is attributed to a cut in Nigeria's banking sector (it is estimated that in the heat of the global crisis, about US$5 billion in international bank credit lines had been pulled from Nigeria[4]). There were also considerable reduction in Ghana, Kenya, Tanzania, and Uganda. Additionally, syndicated bank lending commitments declined in South Africa. Other reasons that underline the importance of developing a local market for private infrastructure financing are: the foreign exchange risk associated with borrowings in hard currency against local currency revenue streams from PPP projects; high cost of international finance resulting from high country risk premiums and foreign exchange hedging; the importance of using infrastructure investments to improve the long-term capacity of local financial markets; and finally, financing smaller projects that would not attract international finance.

The subsections that follow highlight the characteristics and challenges facing existing sources of private infrastructure financing. These main potential sources of local financing are categorized as follows: (i) local commercial banks, (ii) pension funds, (iii) insurance funds, and (iv) capital markets. It is noteworthy that findings from this section support the conclusions by Irving & Manroth (2009) which shows that local financial markets in SSA countries remain underdeveloped, shallow, and small in scale, highlighting the role of Official Development Assistance (ODA) as a source of financing in Africa. The study goes on to suggest the need for the development of appropriate regulations for local institutional investors to enable their participation in infrastructure financing.

Local Commercial Banks

The size of local commercial banks is small relative to the levels of financing required for large infrastructure projects. A great segment of the population in the countries in this study is extremely poor and does not have sufficient financial resources that enable significant savings. Figure 2.2 plots private credit in US$ billions and as a proportion of GDP. The data confirms the small size of the banking sector marking a maximum private credit stock amounting to US$65 billion (38 percent of GDP) for Nigeria. This compares

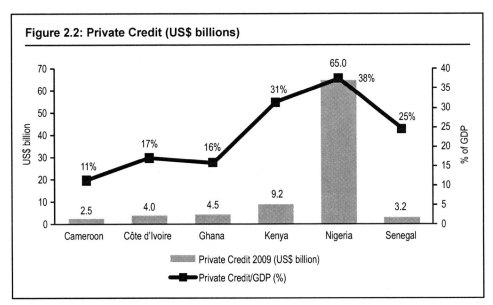

Figure 2.2: Private Credit (US$ billions)

Source: Private credit data for 2009 (Ghana 2008) is computed as the deposit money banks' or institutions'' claims on private sector; from the IFS December 2010 Country Reports; GDP of the corresponding year from the WDI.

with three benchmark countries in which these figures mark 81 percent (US$131 billion), 51 percent (US$632 billion), and 77 percent (US$220 billion) in Chile, India, and South Africa, respectively. Furthermore while not of immediate relevance, single borrower limits, due to the small sized net worth of banks, also bind a single bank's exposure to PPP projects (see table 2.2 for single borrower limits applicable for the largest bank in each of our sample countries).

Additionally banks have a limited capacity to provide long-term infrastructure financing as a result of the asset-liability mismatch between long-term financing required for infrastructure and short-term deposits. Long term resources can originate from customers' long-term deposits or from resources provided by equity markets or through bond issuances. The availability of long-term resources for banks is a prerequisite for awarding long-term loans. The lack of long-term finance puts pressure on project developers to repeatedly refinance. Table 2.2 shows that the longest loan tenors are approximately five years, with very rare exceptions surpassing this tenor. With an average PPP concession duration being 25-30 years, commercial banks are not able to raise such tenors from their deposits that are of short-term nature and are commonly tied for only one year across all the sample countries. It may be worth examining the role of using behavioral maturity of deposits for asset-liability mismatch calculations, as opposed to only their contractual maturities. Furthermore, because of a limited corporate bond market (further discussed in the Local Capital Market section of this report), commercial banks are not able to raise significant long-term financing against their own balance sheets.

Table 2.2: Country Statistics on the Banking Sector

	Cameroon	Côte d'Ivoire	Ghana	Kenya	Nigeria	Senegal
Longest Credit Tenors[5]	5 years (96% of loans are 5 years or less)	5 years (95% of loans are 5 years or less)	5 years (rare exception of 7 years)	5 years (rare exceptions of 15 years)	7 years (rare exceptions of 15 years)	5 years (95% of loans are 5 years or less)
Longest Local Currency Government Bond Tenor	N/A	5 years	5 years	25 years	20 years	5 years
Year of Issue	N/A	2009	June 2007– Dec 2007	June 2010	July 2010	July 2005
Bond Coupon Rate	N/A	6.95%	13.67% -15%	11.25%	10.00%	5.50%
Single Borrower Limit (% of Net Worth)	45%	75%	25%	25%	20%	75%
Single Borrower Lending Limit for the Largest Bank, (in US$ millions)[6]	30.54	106.44	35.28	73.70	471.52	107.96

Source: For government bonds information: Bloomberg December 2010, government central banks, and stock exchanges; for single borrower limits: the authors' interviews with banks; and for banks' net worth data: the banks' balance sheets.

Furthermore the underdeveloped government bond market does not allow for developing yield curve benchmarks necessary for commercial banks to price long-term debt in local currency. The inability to price credit risk because of the lack of a reliable government yield curve is a fundamental obstacle to the nongovernment bond market. Notwithstanding this general condition, some governments such as Kenya and Nigeria have made admirable progress in lengthening the maturity of government bonds to reach 20 and 25 years (table 2.2). However even in these instances, the illiquidity of these bonds due to underdeveloped secondary bond markets remains a further limitation and key consideration in the further development of a robust bond market, as will be discussed in a subsequent section.

The lack of experience of local commercial banks in project financing also contributes to the low capacity of local banks to support projects with long-term financing. PPPs typically rely on commercial banks for funding in many countries. As noted in figure 2.1 (and Infrastructure Investor (2010)) banks are not best suited to be long term holder of infrastructure debt. However they have a critical role to play in the construction period of a PPP project. Local banks in the sample countries are unfamiliar with limited recourse financing structures such as: lending to a SPV and assessing and managing PPP risk, in particular construction risk, offering grace periods, creating appropriate security structures, and the associated inter-creditor arrangements/syndications.

Some countries such as India have taken several measures in the banking sector to increase the availability of funds to infrastructure projects.[7] India has sought to foster infrastructure funding, including measures to promote more long-term deposits and to develop the government bond market and its yield curve. More recently the Reserve Bank of India initiated a number of regulatory concessions for infrastructure finance, such as: (i) allowing banks to enter into take-out financing arrangement; (ii) freedom to issue long-term bonds by banks for financing infrastructure; (iii) adjustment of single and group borrower limit to allow for additional credit exposure in the infrastructure sector; (iv) flexibility to invest in unrated bonds of companies engaged in infrastructure activities within the overall ceiling of 10 percent; (v) excluding the promoters' shares in the SPV of an infrastructure project to be pledged to the lending bank from the banks' capital market exposure; and (vi) permitting banks to extend finance for funding promoter's equity where the proposal involves acquisition of share in an existing company engaged in implementing or operating an infrastructure project in India. These policy changes have been recent, so it is not yet possible to assess the impact they have had on Bank engagement and balance sheet exposure to infrastructure financing.

In this sample of countries a few local commercial banks have been involved in infrastructure project financing. For example in Nigeria, the *Lekki-Epe Express Toll Road*, which reached financial close in 2008, was able to mobilize a 15-year loan from Stanbic's IBTC-Nigeria in local currency for NGN 2 billion (US$13.4 million) at a fixed interest of 13.9 percent and with a moratorium on principal repayments of four years. This deal was also supported by other local banks, namely: First Bank, United Bank for Africa, Zenith Bank, Diamond Bank, and Fidelity Bank which provided a total loan value of NGN 9.4 billion ($60.6 million) for a tenor of 12 years.[8] Another example is in Senegal. The *Dakar-Diamniadio Toll Road* reached financial close in November 2010. The concessionaire Eiffage was able to tap on local credit from the Senegalese bank, The Banking Company of West Africa-CBAO, which provided approximately US$10 million, with a 13.5-year tenor, and around 10 percent fixed interest rate. This amounts to 10 percent of the total debt of the project. Furthermore, the government of Senegal is financing 76 percent of the total investment cost of this project estimated US$539 million, with support from International Finance Corporation, (IFC), African Development Bank (AfDB), and Agence Française de Développement (AFD)[9].

Pension Funds

Pension funds in countries with fully funded pension systems are a potential investor for infrastructure financing. The risk-averse, long-term nature of pension funds fits with the long-term nature of infrastructure cash flows. The increasing role of the pension industry in financing infrastructure is regarded as a win-win situation. On the one hand, pension funds offer local long-term financing, particularly crucial when capital markets are underdeveloped. On the other hand, infrastructure investments offer pension funds long-term yields, higher and stable returns that are linked to inflation, and risk diversification.[10]

However, there are common challenges to mobilizing pensions, some of which are associated with particular features of infrastructure projects. Pension funds typically require listed securities with good credit rating (for example, must achieve at least a local "A"). Most pension funds in SSA do not have staff experienced in PPPs; lack sufficient staff to actively manage lending; and are prone to selection bias based on political priorities. Furthermore, there are characteristics particular to Greenfield infrastructure investments that make it challenging for pension funds to get involved: these projects being untested (and so have low credit rating unless wrapped); many projects cannot be listed; they have complex structures; and must be managed actively particularly in the construction period.

While some pension fund investment regulations allow for investment in infrastructure projects, to date no investments have been made. Figure 2.3 shows the size of pension assets under management in Ghana, Kenya, and Nigeria both in USD values and as a proportion of GDP. Below the investment guidelines for Ghana, Kenya, and Nigeria are described.[11]

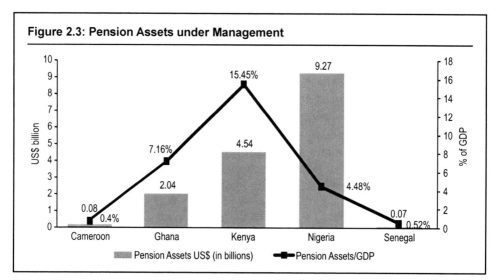

Figure 2.3: Pension Assets under Management

Source: Kenya Financial Sector Assessment Program report (2010); Ghana SSNIT Annual Report (2008); Nigeria Pension Commission—PENCOM Annual Report (2010); Kenya Retirement Benefit Authority (RBA) March 2010 Newletter.

▨ For *Ghana* the following benchmarks are the *target* asset allocations for the SS-NIT, currently the main provider of pensions in Ghana: listed equity (27 percent), unlisted equity (4 percent), corporate bonds (5 percent), government bonds (3 percent), municipal bonds (1 percent), corporate lending (12 percent), sovereign lending (8 percent), municipal lending (1 percent), syndications (2 percent), treasury (15 percent), study loans (2 percent), alternative investments (real estate (15 percent), private equity (3 percent), Economically Targeted Investments (2 percent))

▨ For *Kenya* the following investment asset *ceilings* apply: cash/demand deposits (5 percent), fixed deposits (30 percent), fixed income-private (30 percent), government securities (70 percent), quoted shares in EA and CIS (70 percent), unquoted equity (5 percent), offshore investments (15 percent), immovable property (30 percent), guaranteed funds (100 percent), and any other investments (5 percent).

▨ For *Nigeria* the following investment asset *ceilings* apply: government securities (100 percent for FGN, 30 percent for states); corporate bonds /debt (30 percent); money market instruments (35 percent); ordinary shares (25 percent); open and closed funds (5 percent). Noteworthy that the National Pension Commission (PENCOM) in December 2010 released its revised regulations for Pension Fund Investments which introduce and provide guidelines for infrastructure funds/projects as a new asset class for pension fund investments[12].

To date only Kenya pension funds have been indirectly involved in infrastructure financing through investments in the bond issuance of Kenya Electricity Generating Company (Kengen) and in the telecom company Safaricom. It is worth mentioning that in the case of Ghana, SSNIT is among the nine investors of the Pan African Infrastructure Fund, which was established in 2007 to play a critical role in assisting African economies to meet the capital requirements in financing infrastructure investments. SSNIT's contribution was US$10 million of the total raised US$625 million. Other overseas investments in infrastructure related funds by SSNIT include Emerging Capital Partners (ECP), a manager of six private equity funds that invest in Africa which includes AIG Africa Infrastructure Fund; and the Canadian Investment Fund for Africa.

With regards to Cameroon, Côte d'Ivoire and Senegal, the pension schemes employed in the West African Economic and Monetary Union (WAEMU) zone and in francophone Africa in general are the unfunded pay-as-you-go pension schemes. Under this setup retirement contributions are paid by the active population, which is different from the fully funded model used in Ghana, Kenya and Nigeria whereby the active population saves today for its future retirement money. As such, the size of pension funds for the francophone sample countries is negligible.

There are efforts to mobilize pension funds for infrastructure financing across some developing countries. Pension funds in developed countries such as Australia, Canada, and the UK are considered leaders in the field of investing in infrastructure via private equity funds or sometimes directly. Additionally a number of developing countries have ventured in this field. Chilean private pensions generally invest in infrastructure bond that are 100 percent guaranteed by insurance policies issued by international insurance companies. In Peru in 2000, the investment framework was adjusted to increase pension funds investment in infrastructure (see box 2.1 for a snapshot of pension investments in

---

Box 2.1: Pension Funds and Investments in Infrastructure in Latin American Countries

Pension fund investment in infrastructure has taken two forms: (i) Indirect Investment, which is through investments in fixed income or equity assets in companies tied to the construction or management of infrastructure projects, and (ii) Direct Investment through project finance or PPPs where the pension fund acquires assets that are linked to the return of the project. The table below provides a breakdown of these investments across four countries and the associated legal limits for direct investments in infrastructure.

	Indirect Investment		Direct Investment		Legal Limit on Direct Investment
	US$ Billion	% of Portfolio	US$ Billion	% of Portfolio	% of Portfolio
Chile	9.9	9.17%	1.9	1.8%	No Limit
Colombia	4.4	17.10%	0	0%	No Limit
Mexico	5.5	6.9%	0	0%	10.7%
Peru	2.4	11.5%	0.7	3.3%	No limit

Source: BBVA 2010.

---

infrastructure). In 2009, pensions participated in the creation of an Infrastructure Investment Fund and Infrastructure Investment Trust.[13] Private pension funds are active in the Korean PPP market, in addition to other countries such as Singapore, Malaysia, and China, which have also used pensions for infrastructure investment.[14] Furthermore the Indian finance minister has recently acknowledged the country's needs to encourage long-term investment from the pension and insurance sector in infrastructure space to bridge the deficit.[15]

The OECD encourages pension participation in infrastructure. A recent OECD study examining the role of governments in responding to infrastructure challenges specifically highlighted the role of the private sector.[16] Notably, the OECD presented 17 principal policy recommendations, including: (i) encouraging investment by pension funds and other large institutional investors, and (ii) examining the legal and regulatory framework conditions with a view to encouraging the emergence of fresh sources of capital and new business models for infrastructure. Furthermore, the *OECD Guidelines for Pension Fund Asset Management* (2006) can be read to be broadly supportive of pension fund investment in infrastructure. Inderst (2009) provides a list of potential steps that can be undertaken by governments regarding enhancing the investment environment and removing regulatory barriers to help infrastructure developers tap into pension funds (box 2.2).

Insurance Funds

Similar to pension funds, infrastructure investments fit with the payout schedule of life insurance policies. The data is scarce on country experiences in mobilizing insurance funds for infrastructure financing. In Barbados the National Insurance Board, a corporate body that runs the social security scheme, owns 23 percent of Light & Power Holdings. Similarly the National Insurance Corporation in Saint Lucia owns 16.79 percent of the Saint Lucia Electricity Services Limited. Other countries have modified their insurance regulations to allow for infrastructure investment, for instance the Chinese Insurance

---

Box 2.2: Potential Steps for Governments to Tap Financing for Infrastructure from Institutional Investors

---

Enhance the investment environment

- Decide on the utility and nature of potential private sector involvement
- Provide a sound institutional and regulatory environment for infrastructure investment, including facilitating access to capital markets through the phasing out of unnecessary obstacles to capital movements and restrictions on access to local markets
- Ensure public and institutional support for the project and choice of financing
- Make the cooperation between the public and private sectors work by promoting transparency and appropriate contractual arrangements
- Promote private partners' responsible business conduct
- Remove regulatory barriers
- Promote the prudent person standard of investment
- Remove unnecessary or overly restrictive quantitative investment limits (asset category ceilings, prohibitions on investing in unlisted, overseas assets, etc.)

Others

- Support stronger efforts in independent data collection and objective information provision in the field of infrastructure investment
- Recommend upgrade of national and supranational statistical data collection with a view to better capture infrastructure (and other alternative asset classes)
- Promote higher transparency standards in private equity vehicles and direct investments
- Recommend the establishment of international guidelines for performance and risk measurement of infrastructure (and other alternative) investments
- Encourage the study of more advanced risk analysis beyond the traditional measures, including the specific risks of infrastructure. Advice against a supervisory approach that creates false certainties in risk management
- Encourage improvements in knowledge and understanding of pension fund stakeholders and supervisors on infrastructure assets.

Source: Inderst, G. (2009).

Regulatory Commission revised the insurance law in 2009 permitting insurers to invest in infrastructure. Additionally, the Insurance Regulatory & Development Authority in India allows life insurers to invest in long-term infrastructure bonds proposed by the India Infrastructure Finance Company for refinancing Greenfield infrastructure projects.[17]

The size of the life insurance industry is small relative to pension funds for the Anglophone sample countries, contrary to the francophone sample. Figures 2.4 and 2.5 display the size of investments made by the life and non-life insurance industries respectively.[18]

Below are summaries of the insurance funds investment guidelines/regulations. While these regulations seem to allow room for undertaking infrastructure investments, to our knowledge there have been no investments in infrastructure projects to date:

- *Ghana:* The NIC provides guidelines on investment mixes for the industry to ensure that investments of insurance companies are adequately spread. For the life insurance companies, the guidelines stipulate the following investment ceilings: up to 30 percent in listed stocks, 20 percent in unlisted stocks (10 percent for nonlife insurance companies), 20 percent in mutual funds, 10-30 percent in investment properties (0-20 percent for nonlife), and up to 10 percent in invest-

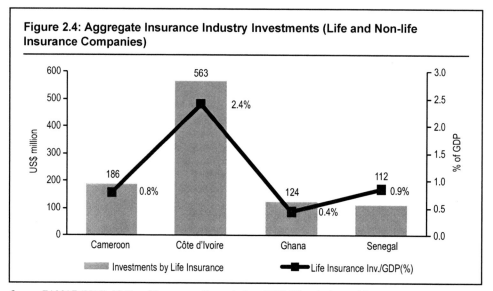

Figure 2.4: Aggregate Insurance Industry Investments (Life and Non-life Insurance Companies)

Source: FANAF (2010); National Insurance Commission (NIC) Nigeria Annual Report (2008); NIC Ghana Annual Report (2008); Insurance Regulatory Authority (IRA) Kenya Annual Report (2009).

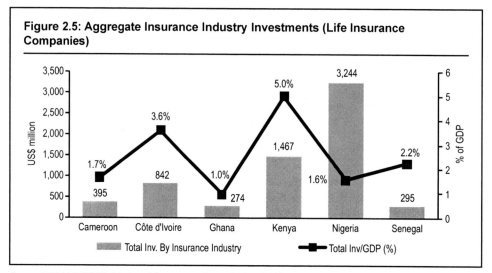

Figure 2.5: Aggregate Insurance Industry Investments (Life Insurance Companies)

Source: FANAF (2010); National Insurance Commission (NIC) Nigeria Annual Report (2008); NIC Ghana Annual Report (2008); Insurance Regulatory Authority (IRA) Kenya Annual Report (2009).

ments approved by NIC. Furthermore, the guidelines stipulate that at any point in time, the ratio of investments to total assets should not be less than 55 percent (that is at least 55 percent of the total assets of the company must be in direct investments, the latter defined as assets that directly earn cash income or appreciate in value over time).

▪ *Nigeria:* The Nigerian Insurance Commission's Operational Guidelines (2010) remain unclear on whether or how investments into infrastructure debt securities or funds can be made. However the guidelines stipulate the following asset allocation ceilings: 50 percent in quoted equities, 10 percent in unquoted equities, 5 percent in leasing equipment, 35 percent of life insurance funds in property (25 percent for nonlife insurance); 5 percent of the total equity investment placed in the security of one company.

- *Kenya:* Investment guidelines are contained inside the Insurance Act. The Act, which was revised in 2010, stipulates the following investment guidelines for long-term issuance business: (i) 20 percent of the total admitted assets (10 percent in case of general insurance business[19]) can in one or more of the following securities: government; prescribed statutory bodies, local authorities, or any other prescribed organizations; (ii) not less than 65 percent (30 percent in case of general insurance business) in one or more of the aforementioned securities; in mortgages on unencumbered immovable property in Kenya; debentures secured by a mortgage on unencumbered immovable property in Kenya; debentures, commercial paper, preference shares, or ordinary shares of public companies whose shares are quoted on the stock exchange in Kenya; instruments of title to immovable property in Kenya; loans on life assurance policies constituting a liability on Kenya business within their surrender values; deposits in banks or financial institutions licensed under the Banking Act; any other prescribed securities; promissory notes, bills of exchange, or other instruments issued by a company incorporated under the Companies Act; and finally, (iii) the remaining balance in investments in Kenya that the insurer seeks fit. Furthermore, insurers can invest up to 5 percent of their total assets in shares or debentures or loans of any one company of group of related companies.

- *Cameroon, Côte d'Ivoire, and Senegal:* All three francophone countries are members of the Inter-African Conference for the Insurance Market (CIMA). The insurance activity in all member countries is regulated by the insurance legislation of the CIMA Code member states set up in 1995. A publication by the Fédération des Sociétés de Droit National Africaines—FANAF (2010) shows corporate investments in life and nonlife corporations for all 14 CIMA member countries (in addition to Burundi, Rwanda and Madagascar) with the Côte d'Ivoire leading with 37 percent of FANAF market followed by Cameroon (17 percent) and Senegal (13 percent) second and third, respectively (Refer to the CIMA Regulations (2007) for the detailed allowed asset allocations for insurance funds).

Local Capital Market

While long-term domestic financing —often available only in local capital markets— is well suited for infrastructure projects, to date this market is limited in Africa. Africa has been less successful in raising project finance in capital markets through corporate bonds compared to other developing regions. Generally, only a few developing countries are equipped with local capital markets that can provide such financing consistently and in significant amounts. These countries are characterized by having larger economies than almost all African countries. Furthermore, their financial markets are sophisticated enough to provide currency forwards and interest rate swaps.[20] Tables 2.3 and 2.4 provide a snapshot of the restrained local capital market in our sample countries. As previously highlighted, addressing the underdeveloped government bond market and developing a yield curve is critical to developing the nongovernment bond market.

Table 2.3: The Local Capital Market

	Cameroon	Côte d'Ivoire	Ghana	Kenya	Nigeria	Senegal
Equity Market						
Stock Exchange	Douala Stock Exchange	Bourse Régionale des Valeur Mobiliers	Ghana Stock Exchange	Nairobi Stock Exchange	Nigeria Stock Exchange	Bourse Régionale des Valeur Mobiliers
	(DSX)	(BRVM)	(GSE)	(NSE)	(NSE)	(BRVM)
Market Capitalization in US$ million [22]	0.35	15.68	11,150	10,970	37,000	15.68
Market Cap/ GDP (%) 2009	0.00%	N/A	42.61%	37.34%	21.39%	N/A
# of Listed Companies	4	38	35	55	215	38
Corporate Bonds Market						
Longest Tenor	5 year[23]	N/A	5 years	8 years	7 years	N/A
Outstanding in US$ million[24] (September 2010)	N/A	N/A	3.9	650	546	N/A
Outstanding/GDP (%)	N/A	N/A	0.03%	2.16%	0.32%	N/A

Source: Axelcium (2010); ASES (2009); and ABSA Capital (2010).

Table 2.4: BRVM Bond Characteristics by Issuer (2003-2009)

Type of Borrowing Organization	Average maturity	Average Interest Rate	Average issue Value (US$ million)
Development Banks	6.3	5.32%	34.18
Commercial Banks	5	6.18%	16.33
Private Sector	6	6.5%	30.71
State Companies	5.75	5.75%	29.23
TOTAL			110.44

Source: Axelcium Report (2010).

A recent analysis of Kenya's capital market outlines concerns likely to also be relevant to the other sample countries. The World Bank technical note (2010) for Kenya, "Nongovernment Bond Market Development Technical Note", highlights a number of obstacles that need to be addressed: *first* to distinguish between the issuance framework between equity and bond instruments with the aim of reducing the stringent disclosure requirement for bonds relative to those required for equity issuers. Relevant to this is adopting a flexible issuance framework that potentially incorporates three avenues for issuing bonds, namely: public offer, private offer, and a hybrid offer.[21] Under the proposed framework, it is expected that many nongovernment bond issuers will choose the hybrid issuance regime, given its less onerous disclosure obligations and ability to easily access key (that is, institutional) investors. *Second,* delink the tax benefits from listing on the exchange to ensure that issuers decide whether to list their bond on the basis of market economics, not a tax advantage. *Third,* the need for adequate regulations for issuing asset-backed securities, which could provide another avenue for infrastructure or housing companies to raise financing. *Fourth* the requirement that issuers have declared after-tax profitability in at least two of the last three financial periods and have audited financial statements for the last three fiscal years. In light of this restriction a new company, especially one created for a specific infrastructure project that has been operating for less than three years, would not be able to meet this requirement and would thus have to forgo the opportunity to access bond financing. This creates a particular challenge for a project finance company, SPV, to issue a bond to finance a new infrastructure project. Finally, there is a need to address the local market and requirements for corporate bond ratings.

Despite the previously highlighted nascent nongovernment bond market, there have been some instances of corporate bonds financing infrastructure. Table 2.5 outlines these bond issues. As displayed, most of these issues have required credit enhancement instruments until recently with the Kengen and Safaricom issuances.

Table 2.5: Nongovernment Bonds Financing Infrastructure

Country	Entity	Tenor	Issue Date	Coupon Rate	Credit Enhancement Instrument/Guarantees
Kenya	KenGen	10 years	2009	12.25%	None
Kenya	Safaricom	5 years	November 2009	12.25%	None
Côte d'Ivoire	Abidjan port Authority	N/A	N/A	6.91%	BOAD & BIDC
Côte d'Ivoire	SOTRA (Société des Transports Abidjanais)	5 years	2007	6.8%	BOAD & BIDC
Senegal	Dakar Port Authority	7 years		6.5%	BOAD

Source: Axelcium Report (2010) and Kenya CMA Bulletin (September 2010).

Sources of International Financing for PPP Projects

International Commercial Banks

International banks have represented a limited financing option for the infrastructure projects of the countries studied. When coming into play, banks propose only short-term financing that is enhanced by risk mitigating instruments from institutional organizations in order to reduce political and commercial risks. Furthermore, these banks cannot lend in local currencies, and the exchange risk borne under a foreign currency loan blocks the access of PPP projects with local currency revenue to international financing.

Almost as a rule, international banks have been operating under the umbrella of a donor or an export credit agency to minimize the loans' political and commercial risks. Examples of projects from the countries under review illustrate that almost all credit mobilized from international banks has been accompanied by credit enhancement mechanisms, including those described below.

   ▨ *The Dakar Container Terminal, Senegal-DP World (US$540 million):* Standard Chartered Bank is involved in the financing of the project. MIGA has issued guarantees totaling €71 million to cover loan and hedging investments by Standard Chartered Bank of the United Kingdom and an equity investment by DP World FZE of the United Arab Emirates.

   ▨ *The Azito Power Project, Côte d'Ivoire (US$233 million):* Paris National Société Générale Bank arranged and syndicated a loan with other international banks. The World Bank provided a Partial Risk Guarantee (PRG) to the private commercial loan for US$30 million against payment defaults due to a default by the state and against nationalization, expropriation, and transfer/convertibility.

■ *The Lekki Toll Road in Lagos, Nigeria (US$380 million):* As previously discussed, Standard Bank is the international commercial financier in this project. Lagos State Government (LASG) provided two 'guarantees/support' with respect to the Lagos Roads Infrastructure Project. The first guarantee is a bank guarantee issued by a commercial bank in favor of Lekki Concession Company (LCC) as a guarantee of LASG's obligations under the Concession Agreement. The second 'guarantee' is not in the true sense a guarantee, but a Federal Support Agreement, issued by the Federal Government of Nigeria in support of the Project. It is an Irrevocable Standing Payment Order (ISPO), whereby the FGN commits that in the event that LCC and the Lenders have any claim against Lagos State under the Concession Agreement and Lagos State does not meet its obligation, the FGN will make deductions from the federal statutory allocations to LASG and pay over these sums to LCC/the Lenders until the sums due are fully paid.

Private Infrastructure Funds

The growth of private infrastructure funds over the last decade in Africa has been damaged by the drying up of liquidity as a result of the financial crisis. A World Bank study on infrastructure funds and facilities in Africa reports an inventory of 45 infrastructure funds that operate in Africa. The total value of capital raised or targeted by these funds is about US$18.9 billion. The information available indicates that investors have committed about US$10 billion of this total to 2009. Most of the infrastructure funds are equity funds, but some provide debt or mezzanine finance.[25]

Outside the telecommunications sector, these private infrastructure funds are not investing significant sums in core infrastructure sectors. This is because of the relatively short and uncomplicated process of telecom project preparation in comparison with other sectors, coupled with the relatively short payback period associated with the sector. This is a significant limitation when considering the positive development impact of core infrastructure. Such finding suggests that IFI involvement in funds and facilities should aim at shifting investment to the basic sectors, such as: transportation, water supply and sanitation, and power.

Donor Infrastructure Funds

The development community has made available a number of funds/facilitates geared towards supporting PPI financing. Listed below are facilities that have supported different aspects of the PPP projects in Africa, including support for technical preparations and financing or providing the relevant enhancing instruments.

■ *The EU-Africa Infrastructure Trust Fund*[26] supports Africa's efforts to identify and address the missing links in existing networks, harmonize transport policies, develop integrated water management, develop cross-border and regional energy infrastructure, and promote efforts to bridge the digital divide. The trust fund currently holds €148 million in pledged contributions. In the light of the unfolding economic crisis, in April 2009 the European Commission called on the member states to target the provision of €500 million in contributions to the trust fund by 2010 and to accept the opening up of the fund to third countries. For its part, the commission will contribute an additional €200 million in 2009-10, tripling its current support. It has also proposed to adapt the trust fund to:

(i) include national infrastructure that forms part of regional networks and (ii) introduce risk guarantee mechanisms. In 2008, four grant operations were approved for a total of €47.8 million, compared to €15.5 million in 2007. Among these projects was a Technical Assistance for €1 million for the Gouina Hydro Power Project (GHPP), the purpose of which is to supply renewable electricity to Senegal, Mali, and Mauritania.

▨ *Private Infrastructure Development Group (PIDG)*[27] is a coalition of donors mobilizing private sector investment to assist developing countries in providing infrastructure vital to boost their economic development and combat poverty. Current members are: the UK Department for International Development (DFID), the Swiss State Secretariat for Economic Affairs, the Netherlands Ministry of Foreign Affairs, the Swedish International Development Cooperation Agency, the International Finance Corporation (IFC)/World Bank, the Austrian Development Agency, Irish Aid, and KfW. PIDG includes a number of facilities that support various aspects of PPI (box 2.3). The country most heavily invested in to date is Nigeria (US$135 million), Kenya (US$76 million), Uganda (US$65

Box 2.3: PIDG Facilities

DevCo is an untied PIDG Facility, managed by the IFC that advises poorer developing country governments on maximizing the benefits from private sector participation in infrastructure.

Emerging Africa Infrastructure Fund (EAIF) is a US$501 million debt fund that aims to address the lack of available long-term foreign currency debt finance for infrastructure projects in SSA. EAIF offers USD and EUR lending to private companies (or soon to be privatized companies) for Greenfield projects or for refurbishment, upgrade or expansion of existing facilities. Examples of projects that were partly financed by EAIF are presented in the table below:

Project	Country	Sector	EAIF investment
Tema Single Mooring Point	Ghana	Transport	US$12 million (loan): Total project US$ 58 million
MTN	Nigeria	Telecom	US$10 million : Total Project US$ 200 million
Celtel	Nigeria	Telecom	US$35 million (loan): Total financing package is US$350 million
Zain Communication	Ghana	Telecom	USD17.5 million (loan): Total project cost is$523 million
Helios Towers Nigeria	Nigeria	Telecom	US$19 million (loan): Total syndicated loan is US$250 million
AES Sonel	Cameroon	Power	US$30 million (loan): Total project US$75 million
Rabai Power	Kenya	Power	Euro 22.57 million
Olkaria III	Kenya	Power	US$15 million

Source: http://www.emergingafricafund.com/.

Guarantco is a facility that provides local currency guarantees to infrastructure projects in low-income countries to mitigate credit risks for local lenders, promoting domestic infrastructure financing and capital market development.

InfraCo Africa is an infrastructure development facility that has been designed to assume the risks and costs of early-stage project development in the lower income countries in Africa.

Infrastructure Crisis Facility– Debt Pool (ICF-DP) is a facility that provides direct bridging finance to infrastructure projects in emerging economies that have been put in financial distress as a result of the financial crisis.

Technical Assistance Facilities (TAF) is a pool of funding within the PIDG Trust to assist PIDG facilities and Affiliated Programs in supporting capacity building and identifying potential investment opportunities.

Source: http://www.pidg.org/.

million), India (US$55 million), and Ghana (US$36m). Worldwide US$204 million has been invested in telecoms, followed by energy/power (US$171 million), industry (US$147 million), and airports (US$39 million).

Sovereign Wealth Funds and Other Public Entities

Another potentially significant source of equity and/or debt capital for core infrastructure is Sovereign Wealth Funds (SWFs). The total assets of SWFs that have strategic interests in Africa include funds from the Middle East, China, and India which have become important players in African infrastructure projects. There is substantial appetite from SWFs in Africa to support foreign country mineral and raw material requirements, as seen with China's successful efforts in locking up deals in the oil and gas sector and in providing substantial transport infrastructure funding. Middle East SWFs are also active in both the physical and social infrastructure sectors. One expects these trends to continue in the near future, but may slow down initially as some of the SWFs restructure their portfolios and investment strategies damaged by the global financial crisis. Several of the SWFs had considerable losses in their global financial sector investments as a result of the crisis but remain active exploring infrastructure opportunities in Africa.

Some of the SWFs and Public Entities active in Africa are described below.[28]

- *China-Africa Development Fund (CADFund)*—introduced in 2007, CAD Fund is essentially an equity fund, investing in Chinese enterprises with operations in Africa in the fields of agriculture and manufacturing industries, infrastructure (electric power and energy, transportation, telecommunications, and water), and natural resources (oil, gas, minerals). Currently more than 30 percent of the projects tendered by the World Bank and AfDB have been completed by Chinese contractors, of which a significant share is supported by the CAD Fund. In January 2010, Nasdaq reported that CAD Fund invested nearly US$540 million to support 27 projects in Africa that are expected to lead to total investments of about US$3.6 billion by Chinese companies in the continent.

- *China Investment Corporation (CIC)*—established in 2007, CIC is a wholly state-owned Chinese investment institution with the mission of making long-term investments that maximize risk-adjusted financial returns for the benefit of its shareholders. CIC and the CAD Fund together are the lead SWF investing in infrastructure in Africa.

- *Export-Import Bank (Eximbank) in China*—although not a SWF, Eximbank China is a government-owned policy bank, is an alternative mechanism by which foreign governments finance infrastructure development in Africa. Through providing concessional loans, China Eximbank bank is supporting about 300 projects in Africa, more than 79 percent of which are in infrastructure. Based on World Bank figures it is estimated that Chinese financial commitments to African infrastructure projects rose from less than US$1 billion per year in 2001–03 to around US$1.5 billion per year in 2004–05, reached at least US$7 billion in 2006—China's official "Year of Africa"—then trailed back to US$4.5 billion in 2007.[29] The two largest beneficiary sectors are power (mainly hydropower) and transport (mainly railroads).

- *Dubai International Capital*—Dubai's SWF has made public its plan to invest less in developed western markets and more in local and emerging markets.[30] It is mentioned by Nigerian financial sector observers that Dubai International Capital was contemplating, and may already have executed, a Memorandum of Understanding with the FGN to invest US$1.5 billion in the Nigerian infrastructure sector.[31] It is unclear whether this initiative is separate from a US$16 billion agreement by Dubai World Corporation to develop oil and gas industry infrastructure in the Niger delta, announced in January 2009.[32] By September 2009, there were indications that a Middle Eastern SWF may have committed US$700 million to one or more projects in Nigeria's telecom sector and was still actively interested in the oil, gas, and mining sectors.[33]

Notes

1. Establishing an SPV is a common structure in PPP projects where the SPV is a new stand alone firm that owns and manages the infrastructure assets until the investment costs are recuperated. The SPV is managed by a sponsor, an equity investor responsible for bidding, developing, and managing the PPP project. SPV provide a way to funding against the cash flow of the project and ring fence the proceeds. This structure can be regarded advantageous to investing in corporations, where inventors expose themselves to all business activities of the firm, including those that do not relate to the specific infrastructure project being considered.

2. PPIAF Gridline Notes (2006).

3. This compares with S&P and Fitch Investment Grade ratings for countries where PPPs have played a larger role, such as: South Africa (BBB+;BBB+), Chile (A+;A) and India (BBB-;BBB-).

4. February 16, 2009, as posted at http://allafrica.com/stories/200902160005.html.

5. For the WAMEU countries, issuance of BOAD also acts as a benchmark for Senegal and Côte d'Ivoire. BOAD latest issuance was in 2009, a 7-year bond with a coupon of 3.26 percent. BOAD has been issuing 7-year bonds since 2003 almost annually.

6. These figures are based on the net worth of the largest bank (in terms of assets) in the respective countries namely, International Bank of Cameroun for Savings & Credit (BICEC) in Cameroon, Société Génerale de Banque en Côte d'Ivoire (SGBCI) in Côte d'Ivoire, Ghana Commercial Bank (GCB) in Ghana, Kenya Commercial Bank (KCB) in Kenya, First Bank of Nigeria (FBN) in Nigeria, and CBAO Groupe AWB in Senegal. Net worth is used a proxy for Tier I capital.

7. Address by Dr. K. C. Chakrabarty, Deputy Governor of the Reserve Bank of India, at the 13th Financial Services Convention of Bombay Management Association, Mumbai, 5 February 2010. (speech on the Web site of the Reserve Bank of India- February 2010): www.rbi.org.in/SCRIPTS/BS_SpeechesView.aspx?Id=468.

8. The full structure of this deal is such that the Total Senior Debt to Equity ratio was 77.79 percent to 22.52 percent. Total senior debt package is as follows: NGN 11 billion (Stanbic IBTC & Standard Bank London: 39.29 percent of the total debt package); NGN 9.6 billion (AfDB); NGN 9.4 billion (Syndicate of Nigerian banks); NGN 3.5 billion (Standby Debt from Nigerian banks). Mezzanine Debt of NGN 5 billion provided by the Lagos state government in addition to NGN 5.318 billion in Shareholder Loans and NGN 1 billion in Standby Equity.

9. Notably $105million has been provided by IDA which includes support to safeguard related work.

10. OECD/IOPS Presentation in Kenya(2008).

11. For Nigeria: Nigeria Pension Guidelines October 2008. For Kenya: Retirement Benefit Authority (RBA) presentation (2007). For Ghana: SNITT Revised Draft Asset Allocation-AUM Estimate as at December 2009.

12. http://www.detail-solicitors.com/index.php?section=news&cmd=details&newsid=25

13. BBVA (2010).

14. Asia-Pacific Economic Cooperation Presentation (June 2010).

15. "Pension Funds Could Invest In infrastructure, As India seeks to expand financing," March (2010) from: http://www.allbusiness.com/banking-finance/financial-markets-investing-funds/14081408-1.html.

16. OECD (2007).

17. http://economictimes.indiatimes.com/personal-finance/insurance/insurance-news/Life-insurers-may-get-to-invest-in-infra-bonds/articleshow/6065567.cms.

18. Data breakdown for the investments of the life and non life insurance companies for Kenya and Nigeria is not available. The breakdown available for Kenya is for total premiums collected in 2009 where the Life insurance business accounted for 57.3 percent of total premium. For Nigeria, a breakdown is available for the total industry assets where the life insurance industry accounted for 32 percent of total assets, the latter estimated at NGN 552 billion (US$4.7 billion), in 2008.

19. Based on the Kenya Insurance Act, "general insurance business" means insurance business of any class or classes not being long-term insurance business.

20. PPIAF Gridline (2006).

21. Public Offer—an offer issued to the public with no limitations on denomination size and number or type of investors, essentially allowing all types of investors, including retail, to participate and subject to full prospectus disclosure as well as ongoing disclosure obligations. Private Offer—an offer placed directly with a small number of qualified investors (defined based on international best practice0). Hybrid Offer—an offer exempt from full prospectus but subject to ongoing disclosure obligations.

22. Data for: Cameroon, Ghana, Kenya, BRVM (Côte d'Ivoire and Senegal) is from the ASEA Yearbook (2009). Data from Nigeria is from ABSA Capital (2010).

23. The only bond issue is the IFC bond.

24. For Senegal and Côte d'Ivoire, the data available on the bond market are presented in table 2.4; for Kenya: from the Capital Market Authority (CMA) Statistical Bulletin (September 2010), for Ghana: from the GSE, for Nigeria: from the ESMID (2010).

25. World Bank (2009).

26. http://www.eib.org/projects/publications/eu-africa-infrastructure-trust-fund.htm.

27. http://www.pidg.org/.

28. NEPAD-OECD (2008).

29. Foster, Chen and Pushak (2008).

30. Robertson (2008). http://business.timesonline.co.uk/tol/business/industry_sectors/banking_and_finance/article5247826.ece.

31. Efforts to confirm with FGN representatives that such an MOU is either contemplated or have already been executed have been unsuccessful.

32. http://www.ameinfo.com/181314.html.

33. Cochran (2009).

CHAPTER 3

The Legislative and Institutional Framework

A sound legislative and institutional framework conducive to PPPs that ensures government commitment, transparency, predictability, and coherence, is a major determinant of private investor engagement in PPPs. Consequently, essential to a successful and sustainable PPP program is designing the relevant policies, laws, and regulations that provide accountable rules, mechanisms, and procedures to govern the development and monitoring of contracts between the public and the private sector. This is also the case with the procurement ascribed for PPPs and requiring government effectiveness in establishing standard competitive tendering and bidding procedures. Putting such systems in place, particularly in developing countries where investors' confidence is weak, is often essential for the market to grow in any sustained way.

To complement adequate legislation, the supporting institutional framework needs to be in place. Certain functions need to be addressed in a PPP program, such as: quality control of processes and project implementation; policy formulation and coordination; technical assistance for PPP projects; standardization and dissemination of contracts; and PPP promotion and marketing.[1] While having a PPP unit is neither a pre-requisite nor a guarantee for successful PPPs, a number of countries have established units as a means to facilitate and manage infrastructure investments, such as Egypt, South Africa, Nigeria, Turkey, Senegal, Korea, as well as UK, Australia and Canada. However, the location, mandates, and governance of such units have varied country by country. For instance, in the UK the PPP unit, now re-established as Infrastructure UK (IUK), is mandated with two key functions: (i) strategic development of "cross-cutting approach to the planning, prioritization, and enabling of investment in infrastructure"; and (ii) support the delivery of major infrastructure projects where there is capital investment from the public sector. The PPP unit in Australia, Partnership Victoria-PV, is mandated to provide information and guidance, project advice, and contract development and monitoring.[2] Furthermore, the PPP unit location can vary ranging from inside the government such as for IUK or outside the government, such as the publicly-owned provincial level corporation Partnerships British Columbia in Canada and the Private Infrastructure Investment Management Center—PIMAC—in Korea. It is equally important that adequate incentive structure be in place to ensure that line ministries own and buy into the PPP institutional framework. This is a critical condition for the success of PPPs.

The main elements of the frameworks across the sample countries in this analysis vary. Each country is at a different stage of developing and/or strengthening its PPP enabling environment, from setting up proper institutions to develop and manage PPPs, to enacting legislation that will permit private sector participation in public service de-livery, to closing PPP transactions. Table 3.1 outlines the PPP institutional and legislative environment in each of the six countries. This is followed by a summary of each country's recent PPP policy and institutional development efforts.

Table 3.1: PPP Legislative and Institutional Environment

	Cameroon	Côte d'Ivoire	Ghana	Kenya	Nigeria	Senegal
PPP Unit	Council for the Implementation of Partnership Contracts (CARPA)[3]	None	PPP Advisory Unit (PAU) and Project Finance and Analysis Unit (PFA)	A PPP Secretariat to the PPP Steering Committee, the latter being a cabinet-level body (not a unit)	Infrastructure Concession Regulatory Commission (ICRC)	A number of entities (National Agency in charge of Investment and Major Works Promotion (APIX); Directorate in Charge of Support to the Private Sector (DASP) [4]; & the Infrastructure Council)
Location of the PPP Unit	Under the Prime Minister	None	Under the Public Investment Department (PID) in the MoFEP	Under the MoF	Under the Presidency	APIX is under the Head of State, DASP is in the MoF; and the Infrastructure Council is an independent body.
PPP Supporting Legislation	An act in 2006 and a decree in 2008 setting the regime for partnership contracts.	None	PPP Guidelines (2004); PPP Law (in progress, expected in 2011); PPP Policy (in draft, 2011);	Kenyan Public Procurement and Disposal (PPP) Regulations (2008)	ICRC Act (2005); PPP Policy (2009); PPP Regulations (in draft, 2011)	CET law (BOT Law) 2004

Cameroon

▨ *Legislative Framework*: In late 2006 Cameroon introduced a legislative and regulatory framework with respect to PPP contracts—two acts and two decrees regulating partnership contracts. Namely: an act in 2006 set the general regime for partnership contracts; (ii) decree in 2009 addressed the enforcement modalities for the previously mentioned act; (iii) an act in 2008 set the tax, financial, and accounting regimes applicable to partnership contracts ; and (iv) a presidential decree in 2008 dealt with the planning and functioning principles of the Support Council for the Implementation of Partnership Contracts (CARPA).

▨ *Institutional Framework:* Cameroon has set up a PPP-dedicated institution, the CARPA, by a presidential decree (2008) that describes the structure and functions of CARPA. The council's remit is for CARPA to contribute, by way of its expertise, to the creation and renewal of public infrastructure and equipment, as well as to the enhancement of the public service standards. These projects are to be implemented on a partnership contract basis. Among CARPA's responsibilities is: supporting project feasibility studies, attending deal negotiations, reviewing progress of the partnership contracts, appraising projects, training national expertise, developing legal and technical instruments for proper implementation of partnerships, and analysis of projects. The guidance committee of CARPA was officially nominated in March 2009 by the prime minister.

Côte d'Ivoire

▓ *Legislative and Institutional Framework:* The conflicts that have shaken the country over the last decade, and more recently following the 2010 elections, have prevented Côte d'Ivoire from focusing on the establishment of a legal and institutional framework more conducive to PPPs.

Ghana

▓ *Legislative Framework:* Following diagnostic work completed in 2010 that assessed key policy, legal, regulatory, and institutional structures with respect to developing a PPP Program, the government prepared a PPP Policy that is scheduled for approval in the first half of 2011. This policy will replace the PPP 2004 Guidelines and lead also to the preparation of a PPP law and the associated regulations. These new pieces of legislation will address the key binding constraints in the current enabling environment for the government with regard to the lack of PPP procurement procedures, systematic project appraisal and development processes, unaccounted contingent liability management plan, and unclear institutional arrangements both for project development and contract compliance responsibilities.

▓ *Institutional Framework:* In line with institutional framework stipulated in the current draft National PPP Policy, the government has established the Public Investment Department (PID) within the MOFEP to provide the central leadership for the PPP Program. The PID comprises four units including a PPP Advisory Unit (PAU) and Project Finance Analysis team (PFA). The PPP Advisory Unit will be mandated to promote the flow of bankable, viable, and sustainable PPP projects that further the National PPP Policy, while the PFA Unit will serve as the Secretariat to the PPP Approvals Committee and will also undertake and coordinate the initial screening of proposals, and make the appropriate recommendations to the PPP Approvals Committee.

Nigeria

▓ *Legislative Framework:* The Federal Government of Nigeria (FGN) first passed the Infrastructure Concession Regulatory Commission (ICRC) Act in 2005 in an effort to create an independent body to manage and develop PPP transactions. The ICRC was officially inaugurated in November 2008. Thereafter, FGN extended these policy reforms by passing a comprehensive National Policy on PPPs in 2009. The Policy addresses the roles and responsibilities of the ICRC as well as the other key MDAs involved in PPPs. The Policy also outlines a clear process by which proposed PPP transactions are examined upstream to determine their commercial viability. Following the creation of the National Policy on PPPs, the ICRC has also embarked on drafting detailed PPP Regulations that will expand on the provisions set forth in the Policy but that also address missing information such as institutional arrangements between MDAs and PPP procurement procedures.

▩   *Institutional Framework:* The ICRC is the mandated entity under the Presidency to manage and develop PPP transactions. Within the agency there are two units: the PPP Resource Center (PRC) and the Contract Compliance Center (CCC). The former will provide support and advice to the contracting authorities on the development and evaluation of PPP projects Furthermore, it is mandated to harmonize the PPP policies and programs of the federal, state, and local governments. The CCC has the responsibility for overseeing, monitoring, and advising on the implementation of all PPP agreements.

Kenya

▩   *Legislative Framework*: The Republic of Kenya has recently undertaken a number studies/reports: The Consolidation, Strengthening and Harmonization of the Policy, Legal and Institutional Framework for the PPP Program in Kenya (World Bank &IP3 2007); draft Policy Statement on PPPs (December 2010); draft Kenya PPP Operating Guidelines (January 2011); Kenya Regulations: a Report on Legal Enabling Environment for PPPs in Kenya (November 2010). This work addresses the issues and challenges with the existing legal and institutional framework, in addition to other issues that would be essential for a successful PPP program.

▩   *Institutional Framework:* The PPP Regulations establish a Secretariat and a Steering Committee (SC) to oversee PPP policy, project implementation, and the process for selection, preparation, evaluation, and procurement of PPPs. The PPP SC is a high-level committee consisting of the Permanent Secretary to the Treasury (chair), the Prime Minister's Office, the Ministry responsible for Planning, National Development and Vision 2030, the Attorney General, and three other members appointed by the Minister. The PPP SC can claim independence as it does not reside within a particular ministry. Responsibilities of the PPP SC are: spearheading the PPP process and promoting understanding and awareness of PPP; reviewing challenges constraining private sector participation and/ or realization of full benefits expected from PPPs; establishing PPP standards, guidelines, and procedures for conceptualization, identification, prioritization of projects; reviewing liabilities and assessing contingent liability risk exposure; ensuring consistency of projects with national priorities; coordinating with the Public Procurement Oversight Authority to ensure conformity with procurement best practices; and approving PPP projects. The Regulations establish the PPP Secretariat within the Ministry of Finance. This unit serves as the Secretariat to the SC as well as operating as a resource center for best PPP practice. This includes: supporting capacity building for PPP project development, contract monitoring, and acting as the focal reference point for advice on PPPs.

Senegal

▩   *Legislative Framework*: Until 2004, there had not been a proper institutional and regulatory framework for PPPs. However, Senegal has since been involved in many lease contracts. From 2004 on, Senegal introduced an infrastructure-specific regulatory framework for PPPs. The wide-ranging legislative reform is the Build/Operate/Transfer (BOT) Law adopted by the National Assembly on February 13, 2004 (the Construction-Exploitation-Transfert d'Infrastructures dite-

loi CET). This legislation allows Senegal to benefit from formal regulations on PPPs for financing, building, operating, and transferring infrastructure to the private sector. As specified in the CET act, the law applies to all BOT contracts in which the state, local authority, public establishment, or corporation where the state owns a majority share entrusts to a third party (called project operator), all or any of the financing, design, construction, operation and maintenance of pubic assets.

▨ *Institutional Framework:* The principal entities involved in Senegal's PPP are: (i) the Agence Nationale Chargée de la Promotion des Investissements et Grands Travaux (APIX). Set up in July 2000, APIX is chiefly remitted to assist the President of the Republic of Senegal in the design and implementation of the policy established with regard to Investment and Major Works Promotion.. The second key institution is (ii) the Directorate in Charge of Support to the Private Sector. This directorate falls directly under the Ministry of Economy and Finance and fulfills functions that more or less directly relate to PPPs, such as: reviewing all the projects involving PPPs and spurring private sector participation in the capital of privatized public corporations. Finally, the third important institution in PPPs in Senegal is (iii) the Infrastructure Council introduced by the CET 2004 law. This institution, which is not attached to any ministry, acts as an independent body to support and manage the implementation of privately financed infrastructure projects. The Infrastructure Council has two types of competences: the first relates to the selection of a project operator and the second to the management of contractual relations. The Council acts at all the stages of a PPP project life as a consultative body and a dispute-settlement entity.

Complementing the overarching PPP legislation, sector-specific legal and regulatory reforms are necessary for private sector engagement. Currently, many sectors do not have proper legislation that allows the private sector to own or operate public assets. It is important for private investors to know that country laws and regulations encourage private investment and protect their commercial interests. For instance, in the transport sector, international experience demonstrates that the most significant delays associated with competitively tendered toll road PPPs are the result of the lack of detailed right-of-way requirements and standard tolling procedures. Without these policies in place, the private investor is forced to assume risks that render the transaction unappealing. This is particularly true in the context of transactions that rely on user fees to be profitable. In such cases, the lack of tariff policies or the existence of insufficient policies give the investor no idea on the level of tariff, how the tariff can or cannot be collected, or how the tariff is calculated and if can be adjusted. This results in overwhelming risk levels for the private sector.

The following examples from the water sector in Kenya and the transport sector in Ghana illustrate the need for sector polices conducive for PPPs. In Kenya, the Water Act (2002) established several new institutions to develop, maintain, and provide water and sanitation services, namely, the Water Service Boards (WSBs) and the Water Service Providers (WSPs). It also created the Water and Sanitation Regulator, which approves water and sanitation tariffs and adjustments to the tariffs. The Regulations allow the WSB and WSP to recover costs, including any debt required to finance new projects. However, they do not include guidelines to adjust tariffs for equity returns, nor do the Regulations specify whether these are returns on the WSB and WSP investment (return on retained earnings) or returns on equity provided by private project sponsors. A legal opinion is required to determine whether or not WSBs and WSPs, as public companies, can include an equity return in their tariff adjustments given that PPP investors will likely require tariff adjustments to provide a return on their equity investment.

In Ghana, one of the legal obstacles identified by the Accra-Kumasi toll road transaction advisor is the conflicting laws governing the sector. The relevant legislation includes: (i) the Road Fund Legislation, which governs the collection and lodging of tolls; (ii) the Ghana Highway Authority legislation, which gives the right to engage with the private sector; and (iii) the Toll Decree Act, which fixes toll rates. It is unclear whether these institutions can delegate toll collection and control of tariff revenues to a private party and whether creditors can enforce the toll collection and toll tariff clauses in a concession agreement. The advisors for this transaction have recommended that the Ministry of Roads and Highways resolve this matter before preparing the draft concession agreement and tender documents for the project's Request for Proposals. Despite these sector-level constraints, which are common across many countries (Nigeria is also facing constraints in developing toll roads because of the absence of a tolling policy), there have been a few that have moved forward where sector reforms have supported PPP transactions (see box 3.1).

Box 3.1: Examples of Sector Reforms that Supported PPP Transactions in Kenya, Nigeria, and Senegal

Kenya: the most promising PPP projects are Independent Power Plants (IPPs) in the power sector. This is a direct result of the successful reforms Kenya has undertaken toward vertical unbundling of its electricity sector with the Kenya Electricity Generating Company (KENGEN), the government-owned company responsible for power generation, and the Kenya Power and Lighting Company (KPLC), solely responsible for the transmission and distribution of electricity with joint public-private sector ownership. With support from PPIAF, the government of Kenya developed a successful strategy for restructuring the country's power sector to facilitate private sector participation in both generation and distribution. This support made possible government adoption of a new energy policy in 2004, which subsequently led to an initial public offering (IPO) in April 2006 of 30 percent of the shares of Kenya Electricity Generating Company (KenGen). Over US$109 million was raised by the IPO, the largest equity sale in the country's history.

Senegal: the government of Senegal has launched an ambitious infrastructure development program, and has decided to involve the private sector in the design, financing, and construction of new infrastructure projects. Among the major infrastructure projects under development is the implementation of the Dakar-Damniadio toll road facilitating the link between the administrative and economic capital to other cities within Senegal.

The government of Senegal launched wide-reaching reforms in 1995 in the water sector. The reforms consisted of dissolving the state-run water company and creating a new asset-holding company that owned all the fixed assets in the government's name and had a mandate to manage the sector. The distribution and production were delegated to a separate entity, and a private operator was engaged to run the system. The Senegal water sector reform was also facilitated by the strategic use of private finance, both from the private operator (who financed some investments) and from local private banks that provided a line of credit to assist the state asset-holding company with its cash flow.

(Box continues on next page)

Box 3.1 (continued)

Nigeria: the Lekki Epe-Expressway in Lagos has been supported by the new enabling legislation-the Lagos State Roads Law 2004. Under the terms of the concession agreement between the Lekki Concession Company and Lagos State Government, traffic management responsibility rests primarily with Lagos State Traffic Management Authority (LASTMA). LASTMA Law (No.9) of 2004 confirms LASTMA's responsibility for regulating, controlling, and managing road traffic in Lagos State, and for enforcing road traffic laws as well as prosecuting road traffic offenders.

Notes

1. PPIAF Gridlines (2007a).
2. Hahm, J (2010).
3. CARPA: Conseil d'Appui à la Réalisation des Contrats de Partenariat.
4. APIX: Agence Nationale chargée de la Promotion de l'Investissement des Grands Travaux, and DASP : La Direction de l'Appui au Secteur Privé.

CHAPTER 4

A Well-Structured PPP Pipeline

A supply of well structured PPP transactions is a key determinant for the private sector to enter the infrastructure market. The private sector responds well to governments that have thought through a proposed transaction and that have committed to competitively engaging with the private sector. The three principal impeding factors are: (i) lack of coordinated public sector strategies or sound infrastructure plans that guide the prioritization of projects; (ii) absence of systematic public sector approach to upstream project analysis to determine the commercial viability of PPP projects and assess the various aspects of the transactions, such as risk allocation, before engaging with the private sector; and (iii) prevalence of unsolicited bids and the absence of standardized and well-practiced competitive PPP bidding procedures. .

One of the primary reasons for delays in PPP projects is the lack of adequate upstream project development and preparation. Thorough upstream analysis of PPP projects is critical to a project's success. Both prefeasibility studies and full-feasibility studies[1] are needed to analyze the technical, financial, environmental, and social aspects of the project. These studies further address issues such as: if the project is in line with the sector policy; if it achieves value for money (VfM); the responsibilities of the different parties; optimal risk allocation; tariff structure; structure of any government subsidy or other fiscal support needed (also in terms of government assets); in addition to the key terms of the PPP contract. Such sophisticated analysis is associated with legal, technical, and financial advisors. Commonly, the related costs can reach up to 10 percent of the total cost of the project, a cost that is arguably justified in light of the expected efficiency gains from PPPs and thus governments need to internalize these costs as they embark on PPPs as a means for infrastructure provision.[2]

Almost all the PPP transactions reviewed in the countries under study originated from unsolicited proposals. The sponsors of these proposals often provide limited engineering, cost, and demand information to assess financial feasibility. They then market the project to governments in the hope of securing financing. Furthermore, unsolicited bids prevent the public sector from leading the sector dialogue and can thus give way to ad hoc investments that steer from sector strategies. This precludes the government from completing initial financial prefeasibility analysis to determine the extent, if any, of government financial support required to ensure project bankability. These unsolicited proposals are typically procured on a sole source basis which is generally a "least cost-effective" procurement standard. On the one hand, unsolicited bids can provide an avenue by which the private sector—who can have a better eye to spot projects that can fit a PPP model,—can mobilize a project. But the Value for Money determination is often insufficiently assessed. To correct for this, unsolicited bids need to be redirected—to the extent possible—into some form of competitive process (some examples of how this is done are: Swiss challenge, Best and Final Offer, Bid Bonus and Developer's fees).[3]

An underlying factor is the weak human capital and low capacity in governments to develop sound PPP transactions. It is instrumental to have a capable body of public sector counterparts across all key MDAs with the capacity to develop, understand, appraise, and manage PPP transactions. There is a lack of understanding of the general characteristics of PPPs, including key elements such as: realistic project development timeframes, proper transparent tendering and bidding procedures, best practice upstream project appraisal analysis, and fair risk allocation between public and private sectors. This low capacity prevails throughout all levels of the PPP enabling environment, from the regulating agencies to line ministries sponsoring the PPP transactions, and the agencies responsible for the assessing and managing fiscal commitments arising from PPP transactions.

Notes

1. Other terminologies used for these studies are Outline Business Case (OBC) and Full Business Case (FBC), respectively.
2. Dos Santos Senna and Dutra Michel (2008) and Yescombe(2007).
3. See PPIAF Gridlines (2007b)

CHAPTER 5

Risk Allocation and Fiscal Management of PPPs

While PPPs can bring private sector finance, experience, and efficiency to infrastructure service provision at a better VfM than traditional public procurement, government's contribution to the "partnership" often gives rise to fiscal commitments. Under a PPP, the government almost always bears some risk or provides some support that gives rise to an ongoing fiscal commitment. These government contributions are needed to mobilize private investment in a way that achieves Value for Money (VfM) by ensuring that projects are financially viable and by allocating risks well between public and private parties. The fiscal commitments that the government commonly ace[t under a PPP can be categorized into two types: (i) *direct*, where the value and timing of the payment are known (such as annuity or availability payments); and (ii) *contingent*, where the value or timing of the payment depends on some uncertain future event (such as shadow tolls or output-based subsidies, guarantees on particular risk variables such as demand, exchange rate tariff setting; termination payment commitments, and debt guarantees.)

The task of risk assessment and risk allocation is a sophisticated and detailed process that requires tailored skills and expertise. Risk assessment is inherently challenging. For instance on Greenfield transport projects, demand risk is extremely difficult to transfer entirely to the private party given that traffic and demand forecasts cannot be based on any existing trends. Furthermore, the exercise of risk quantification is commonly constrained by the availability of objective data on which cost estimates can be based over the 25-30 years of the project. In Chile, a country with an advanced PPP program, there have been 147 significant renegotiations out of 50 concessions, leading to an estimated renegotiation cost of US$2.8 billion.[1] Generally, allocating risk across the different parties is a complex process that involves too many interfaces all trying to get consensus. In this respect, the quest of trying to fully incorporate all risks can be a tedious process, making it too long to incubate deals, and yet this risk management will be far from perfect. Offering the private investors an attractive risk-sharing contract proposal while balancing out the need to minimize public fiscal liabilities, is the cornerstones of successful PPPs. As previously discussed, this calls for support from experienced transaction advisors during the project preparation process to determine the adequate balanced risk-sharing agreement. Box 5.1 provides a sample of the allocation of risks across the public and private sector.

Box 5.1: The Examples of a Preferred Risk Allocation Matrix

The table below addresses only a sample of all potential risks. The risk allocation matrix is based on best practices and OECD country standards, which may not directly apply to the countries under study given their risk profile and where one would reasonably expect governments to bear a greater proportion of project risk. They are, however, presented here as standards to work toward.

Risk	Definition	Proposed Preferred Risk Allocation
Environmental liabilities existing prior to project	Project site safeguard risks requiring significant remediation costs.	Private, except when: • Project was solicited by the government; and • Cost and time required to conduct a full due diligence (site study) for each bidder are such that the project would be significantly delayed or would deter potential serious bidders—in such case, some risk sharing along the lines of geotechnical site risk could be a solution.
Design	Risk that the design of the facility is substandard, unsafe, or incapable of delivering the services at anticipated cost and specified level of service (often resulting in long-term increase in recurrent costs and long term inadequacy of service).	Private: • Private partner will be responsible except where an express government-mandated change has caused the design defect.
Construction	Risk that events occur during construction that prevent the facility being delivered on time and on cost.	Private, except when: • The event is one for which relief as to time or cost or both is specifically granted under the contract, such as force majeure or government intervention; • In situations where the technical or geological complexity (for example, tunnels) prevents having sufficient and reliable information to measure risk, the government may assume part of the risk.
Exchange rate	Risk that during operation, exchange rates may move adversely, affecting the private partner's ability to service foreign-denominated debt and obtain its expected profit.	Shared: • Government to assume part of it by allowing total or partial indexing of payments to exchange rate; • Private to assume remainder.
Inflation	Risk that value of payments received during the term is eroded by inflation.	Shared: • Government to assume part of it by allowing total or partial indexing of payments to inflation; • Private to assume remainder risk through the methodology adopted to maintain value.
Financing unavailable	Risk that when debt and/or equity is required by the private firm for the project it is not available then and in the amounts and on the conditions anticipated.	Private
Tax changes	Risk that before or after completion the tax impost on the private firm, its assets, or on the project will change.	Private, if and when: • Tax increases or new taxes arising from general changes in tax law. • Government, if and when: • Tax increases or new taxes arising from discriminatory changes in tax law.

(Box continues on next page)

Box 5.1 (continued)

Risk	Definition	Proposed Preferred Risk Allocation
Demand risk	Risk that operating revenues falls below forecast as a result of decrease service volume (i.e. traffic volume, water or power consumption) attributable to an economic downturn, tariff increases or change in consumer habits.	Private, except when: • Uncertainty in demand forecast is such that providing an availability payment element and/or a minimum revenue guarantee is necessary to attract private investment (for example, Greenfield toll road), in which case, the government will share in the risk through an availability payment or a minimum revenue guarantee.
Default and termination	Risk of "'loss" of the facility or other assets upon the premature termination of lease or other project contracts upon breach by the private firm and without adequate payment.	• Private firm will take the risk of loss of value on termination.
Residual value on transfer to government	Risk that on expiry or earlier termination of the services contract the asset does not have the value originally estimated by government at which the private partner agreed to transfer it to government.	• Private partner can incorporate lifecycle maintenance, refurbishment, and performance requirements into the design facility, and can manage these process during the term of the contract.
Force majeure	Risk that inability to meet contracted service delivery (pre or post completion) is caused by reason of *force majeure* events.	Shared: • Private takes risk of loss or damage to the asset and loss of revenue when risk is insurable (for example, earthquake, floods, fire, and drought). • Government takes some risk of service discontinuity both as to contracted service and core service when • risks are uninsurable (i.e., terrorism acts, war, • civil unrest, etc.).
Regulation	Risk that where there is a statutory regulator involved there are pricing or other changes imposed on the private firm that do not reflect its investment expectations.	• Private, except when tariffs or payments are pre-specified in the contract.

Source: World Bank & Castalia (2010)—refer to the report for a full list of risks.

Some countries, such as Korea, have provided significant support and gave in to some private sector demands at the initial stages of implementing PPPs in order to build their program. Countries with a limited PPP track record may want to provide some incentives in risk allocation at the early stage of a country's PPP project cycle. A key factor to the growth of the Korean PPP program can be attributed to Minimum Revenue Guarantees (MRGs) provided by the government. At the start of the PPP process, between 1998 and 2003, the Korean government was generous in its support with MRGs, covering up to 80-90 percent of estimated operating revenues provided for up to 20-30 years of the project. As the PPP program developed, these figures dropped gradually and were revised in 2006 to cover up to 10 years of the project. Furthermore, MRGs support only solicited projects and cover up to 75 percent of the estimated operating revenue during the initial five years, declining to 65 percent in the following five years.[2]

However, if such fiscal commitments are not well managed, the potential advantages of a PPP can erode. A wrong incentive for using PPPs over traditional public procurement is to move public investment off budget and debt off the government balance sheet. As previously noted, PPPs are commonly associated with instruments of government support, implying that governments still bear considerable risks and face potentially large fiscal costs from such projects. Proper valuation, accounting, and reporting of the fiscal implications of PPPs are essential to prevent their misuse. Information on contingent liabilities and guarantees associated with PPP projects should be disclosed in budget documents and government financial statements. In Indonesia, concerns have been raised regarding the role of the Ministry of Finance, which had the chance to intervene in the development of a concession only when it was too late to propose major changes without serious disruption of the investment program. This has led to messy government responses to claims of compensations by investors in the wake of the Asian Crisis, which ultimately crippled many of the projects. Such problems could have been more effectively addressed if the Ministry of Finance housed an expert PPP unit that tracked the fiscal obligations of these deals.[3]

There are no systems in place specifically for managing ongoing fiscal commitments for PPPs among the countries included in this analysis. So far, those commitments have been limited, since these countries have had a few PPP projects, and these projects have in turn required only limited government support. However, as these countries ramp up their PPP programs to provide more infrastructure services, it will be important to fill existing gaps in managing fiscal commitments to those projects—both to ensure these PPPs achieve VfM and to avoid accumulating a high level of exposure that could threaten fiscal and debt stability.

Nigeria had taken the first steps toward developing a Contingent Liability and Fiscal Commitment Management Framework for PPPs. A report is currently being drafted to provide an overview of the FGN's existing exposure under PPPs; propose a framework for managing future commitments and develop an action plan to implement the proposed framework. This work also outlines the approval process for fiscal commitments, documents Outline Business Case and Full Business Case (pre and full feasibility studies) requirements for fiscal commitment approval, and prepares formats and brief accompanying guidance for disclosing fiscal commitments to PPPs.

Notes

1. Engel (2010).
2. Kim, J. (2008) and Yescombe (2007)
3. Irwin, T. and Tanya Mokdad (2009).

CHAPTER 6

Medium-Term Options for PPP Financing

The analysis above outlines the principal PPP financing challenges that confront the six sample countries, noting important differences among them. For instance Nigeria and Kenya have deeper government bond markets and longer yield curves, while Senegal and Côte d'Ivoire are part of a regional stock exchange. All these countries are moving along a path of financial and capital market development, albeit at different speeds and with different orientations. Over the longer term, as the enabling environment (comprising the institutional arrangements and the plethora of sector and procurement policy and legislation) improves and is better able to foster PPP investments, the overall capacity and competence to assess, design, and implement PPP projects deepens, pension, insurance, and corporate bond alternatives for PPP financing will become more prevalent and deployable. Nevertheless significant gaps remain over the short and medium term. This section addresses some of the medium-term options that countries can pursue to help close these gaps while the longer-gestating financial and capital market developments take place. This includes approaches to address: (i) high upfront capital costs, (ii) longer-term domestic financing needs, (iii) specific political (government performance) risk mitigation, and (iv) PPP market failures deriving from country size and specific financing challenges posed by cross-border infrastructure constraints. These four sets of issues are investigated in terms of rationale, delivery mechanisms and, finally, prospective financing sources.

Tackling High Upfront Capital Costs

Much of the core infrastructure in Africa requires significant upfront capital investment to bring it to a point at which a viable flow of commercial returns can be realized. This is broadly true for roads, railways, urban water systems, and much of the power supply chain (particularly generation—IPPs—but this in turn is also dependent on quality of transmission and distribution capacities and performance). This it is not just a supply-side constraint. PPPs will add considerable pressure for governments to move toward cost-recovering commercially based tariffs. However, these pressures need to be balanced against transition considerations (namely, how to have users pay increased tariffs before they see a track record of improved service provision—this being a "willingness to pay" issue) and broader national and social equity considerations that militate against such a tariff structure. This is made more difficult when demand levels are so low that it would require a prohibitively high tariff to reach break-even (this being the "ability to pay" challenge). If the government is going to have to provide public finance to close

PPP project funding gaps, why highlight the upfront capital costs versus the public support that may also be required to make up the downstream revenue flows needed to make the project bankable? The Net Present Value (NPV) of a project costs and revenues and the all important financial (FRR) and economic rates of return (ERR) reduce to single numbers. So why not derive these numbers and then simply set up a public financing solution to make up the shortfall required?

This reflects some specific characteristics of PPP infrastructure markets in Africa. The first is the predominant capital investment share of PPP project costs in both Brownfield and Greenfield investments in Africa, allied to the absence of deep financial and capital markets able to finance these substantial costs over the extended period needed for the private sector to break even. Private investors have frequently highlighted that this is often one of the most overriding factors discouraging entry into the market and, as such, requires particular attention. Second, there are a range of institutional considerations (administrative capacities and incentive effects) embedded in NPV, ERR, and FRR calculations that require specific solution designs in order to effectively address the commercial gap problems that present themselves with many PPPs in Africa. These considerations also suggest a separation of approaches to focus on the upfront capital cost issue. Two options coming out of the dialogue with government and private sector are investigated here: the aforementioned VGF and mezzanine financing arrangements.

Consider first the VGF option, which a wide range of governments often do in one way or another. One of the most formal and structured versions is the India's VGF program implemented at a federal level and managed out of the Ministry of Finance. Other examples of structured VGF mechanisms come from Chile, Colombia, and Mexico. They all have unique features and administrative arrangements that vary to address the specific institutional and political economy issues of each country. In the India model, up to 40 percent (20 percent from the VGF and up to 20 percent from sponsoring ministry/state government) of the total cost of a PPP project can effectively be financed from the VGF.[1] To manage risks, these funds only be accessed only through a competitively bid process and not until the equity for the project is in place and the cash flow model agreed. Only then are VGF funds released in a *pari passu* manner with project sponsor funds. Moreover, for a VGF allocation to be considered for a prospective PPP, upfront assessment work is required. This includes a determination as to whether an investment is a government priority; whether it is justified from an economic viewpoint; and if it is suitable for a PPP structure. This entails confirmation that the project is part of the National Investment Plan, followed by a standard cost-benefit analysis (CBA) to determine the overall economic merits. Then a VfM exercise is carried out to determine if a PPP arrangement can deliver the investment at an overall lower cost and better service quality versus a strictly public financing arrangement. This upstream investment appraisal work is a fundamental first-stage exercise in determining the public merit of an investment and the PPP rationale and to lay the foundation for the detailed PPP project development, structuring, and financing that will then follow.

The India VGF, which was modeled on a scheme first developed by the National Highways Authority of India (NHAI), has, to date, been focused on the road sector and is "normally… in the form of a capital grant at the stage of project construction."[2] This priority for VGF financing appears to reflect the limit placed on the total VGF share of project costs, which means that these funds are most usually fully drawn down during high-cost construction periods where there is no offsetting revenue flow from user revenues. A similar circumstance is anticipated for VGF mechanisms that are under consideration in a number of African countries, even where the ceiling for VGF share is significantly higher than the overall 40 percent permissible under the Indian model. In addition to tackling this major initial barrier to the entry of private investment, there are a number of other incentive issues to consider in structuring the VGF.

Different VGF objectives can be realized in various ways. Take, for instance, a prospective railway PPP. The government has identified this as a priority investment but recognizes that it will require significant upfront capital investment and, taking into consideration willingness to pay when faced also with service competition from the trucking industry, concludes that the required freight rates for this PPP to be commercially viable are infeasible. In view of this, the government decides there is a public good argument in financing a significant portion of this upfront capital investment from the public purse. This can be done using traditional public or PPP procurement approaches. Both options, at a conceptual level, can be considered VGF actions but only the PPP procurement route can really contribute to better PPP market development. There are three key reasons for this: the first derives from the competitive impact that it will have on sponsors, the second derives from the nature of risk mitigation that it provides and the third relates to the incentives that it can create for line ministries to pursue competitive PPP procurement.

Where VGF funding is provided in a competitive process it introduces a cost discipline to the overall project that is absent from the public procurement route that would be uniquely focused only on the capital works to be financed. In the case of India, this is done by awarding the VGF funding to the bidder who submits the proposal for the lowest VGF allocation consistent with the technical, operational, market, and other specifications laid out in the VGF bid documents. Given this market approach and the intent to make VGF available for more than one sector, the VGF is typically administered through the central agency (Ministry of Finance). This serves to ensure that the funds available under a VGF go to the best and most cost-effective proposals. Moreover, as these funds are separate from MDA budgets, it provides incentives for line ministries, which are the government sponsors of the PPPs in the different sectors, to conform to government-wide PPP policy and focus on related eligibility and preparation requirements, with the overall result of better appraised and more market-ready projects.

The other key feature of this version of the VGF is the impact it can have on construction risk. When a government proceeds to complete upfront public investment work, the potential PPP sponsor is left to estimate when the assets can be taken over and when revenue flow will commence. This is likely to require revenue guarantees to cover any hiatus between targeted and actual construction completion that delays service start-up and cuts into projected revenue flow. The VGF that is bid out to prospective PPP sponsors rather than construction firms seeking a public procurement contract would transfer this construction risk to the PPP sponsor. Given this is one of the riskier aspects of any PPP, it is potentially a significant cost savings to public funds.

As noted in a recent World Bank study, construction and operating companies are some of the leading investors and sponsors of PPPs in core infrastructure. [3] One of the competitive advantages in entering these markets comes from the ability of these types of companies to derive construction and project management payments from upfront capital investments. This offsets their investment costs. Not only is this a market advantage over other financing sources where returns are dependent solely on revenue flows from the infrastructure service itself, but it adds to the appeal of a VGF, as access to these funds for construction services rendered effectively reduces their investment costs as the downstream PPP operator. This would not be available with a public procurement contract.

The incentive dimension of the VGF can derive from situating it as a "fund" in a central agency (such as Ministry of Finance) and budgeting it under a separate code vote from the line ministries. This can serve to reinforce that this is additional funding for those line ministries willing to pursue PPP approaches in line with the competitive criteria and procedures laid out. This provides an incentive to line ministries. Moreover, this would also increase leverage over the government agencies to follow transparent and well-defined PPP procurement guidelines. This in turn is a strong positive signal to send to the private sector, together with the additional assurance provided on the predictability and certainty of the funding insofar as it is provided under a separate non-fungible budget line item that can be clearly established in the government's approved "Main Budget Estimates." Market confidence in the VGF can be further enhanced if the government is able to commit funds over the longer term. India has addressed this by capitalizing its VGF with an initial allocation understood to be up to US$10 billion. Brazil mitigated the risk by classifying VGF as an "interest payment," which, in accordance with their budget rules, exempts the VGF from the need to obtain annual legislative approvals. These options are not always available, but efforts should be made to ensure at least a rolling three-year estimate of allocated funding to the VGF. This three-year period projection, which is a more widespread medium-term expenditure planning practice, would effectively cover most anticipated construction periods over which financiers would be exposed and therefore provide some comfort to the private sector on the reliability of the funding. It may also require additional risk mitigation guarantees against government defaults on VGF payments. The VGF estimate would need to be based on some substantive pipeline and project assessment work to identify likely VGF funding requirements. An additional advantage of what is essentially a "vertical fund" is greater ease in its monitoring and evaluation against clearly stated objectives. This in turn will increase its appeal to donor partners looking to provide more program-level support to infrastructure development through PPPs.

Further considerations in structuring a VGF are those of accountability, line ministry ownership, and institutional risk. The targeting of VGF allocations on construction cost components of a PPP provides a greater specificity in the utilization of the funds. This will augment the "accountability" of a VGF and, inter alia, its appeal to prospective "first-mover" donor contributors. It would also reduce potential confusion in the downstream responsibility for the project oversight that would need to come from the line ministry. If there are public transfers required after construction (for example, annuity payments), these can then be financed by the line ministry as part of its ongoing responsibility to manage the concession contract. This has the potential to increase line ministry ownership and engagement with the PPP. Additionally, and finally, it unbundles political risk allowing any guarantees to be provided against VGF payments from the central ministry to be separated from those that may be required against annuity payments made by line ministries. Each country considering a VGF mechanism will need to assess these different determining factors and arrive at the model best suiting its specific institutional situation. As the PPP market evolves and matures, these arrangements should be reviewed and revised to ensure they remain optimally effective.

Another part of the solution could be increased resource to mezzanine financing. Equity is particularly difficult to mobilize in Greenfield situations where there is no recent operational track record on which to project demand and revenue flows and there are limited exit options. Traditional senior debt is also scarce until the revenue generation from a PPP is assured. VGF funds can offset this, but to also provide security to public funding objectives, the VGF usually requires equity upfront. One alternative option is mezzanine, or transitional financing, that seeks rates of return between that of equity and secured debt. The exact hurdle rate will, inter alia, be determined by the extent to which the mezzanine funding is subordinated. Provided the VGF funding treats the mezzanine as an acceptable form of transitional equity, then its relatively short tenor (two- to three-year construction period) and "higher-than debt-returns" may serve to mobilize additional key financing from regional and other financial institutions. This is not a financial product that is significantly in use in African infrastructure financing, but there is potential for an increased role in tandem with the introduction of VGF funds and other complementary financing products, including longer-term local currency financing and more systematic use of guarantee instruments. It offers an alternative to handling difficult-to-mobilize equity and may be a vehicle for international currency denominated debt that, over a more limited timeframe of two-three years with a put/call option can diversify exit options.

This mezzanine investment could also be guaranteed in ways that would not be available to straight equity. The key distinction here is the need to look to hybrid debt/equity instruments and see to what extent they can be deployed to help fill financing gaps to cover the high initial capital start-up costs that cannot be addressed by VGF and equity alone. This is a financing area where international financial institutions with capacity to provide mezzanine and hybrid debt/equity financing could fill a key void. VGF facilities, buttressed as required with guarantees, would further increase attractiveness of this investment option.

Longer-Term Local Debt Financing

The inability of sponsors to effectively match long-term PPP local currency revenue projections with locally denominated debt payments leads to potentially prohibitive foreign exchange risks that cannot be hedged and refinancing costs that are highly vulnerable to macro-instability and political change. Quite simply, if Africa is to build core infrastructure beyond that which generates strong short-term returns (for example, telecommunications) or foreign exchange earnings (ports, some IPP projects), then solutions to long-term local debt market gaps are necessary. The structuring of these solutions will need to take into account some critical market realities if they are to be sustainable and contribute over the longer term to a meaningful yield curve on which broader corporate bond market development can also be built.

As noted earlier, only a few countries in Africa have public bond markets beyond five to seven years. With the exception of South Africa, this is includes only Kenya and Nigeria. Where yields already reach out to 15-20 years, it is possible to price long-term local debt that will not undermine corporate bond market development. For instance, in the case of Nigeria, commercial long-term debt was based on a moving average of 10 and 20-year government bond issues adjusted for commercial risks. This approach would be equally applicable in the case of Kenya. Where the yield curve is not this long, alternative pricing approaches are needed to approximate market conditions. Take the example of a recent housing finance product put in place in Tanzania.[4] In this case the government is on-lending funds to the Tanzania Mortgage Refinance Corporation (TMRC). This requires first that a price be set for the on-lending and then add a mark-up to reflect the TRMC lending rates charged to mortgage lenders (banks and other financial institutions). Consider specifically how in this instance the government prices long-term money to the TMRC in order to foster the sustainable development of this market rather than crowd it out. A benchmark price is required, and this should be derived from the most liquid and deep bond in operation. In the Tanzanian case, this benchmark is derived from taking the six months' average of the most liquid bond rate (182 day T-bill). In order to obtain a representative price for longer term, a maturity mark-up needs to be built into the price to approximate the additional time preference sacrifice it entails. Given a number of factors (as cited by the IMF this includes lack of repo market, shallow primary and nonexistent secondary markets, buy-to-hold investor practices, limited institutional buyers), the current pricing trends of different maturities in Tanzania is anomalous.[5] As an alternative, maturity spreads in the South African bond markets are used as a proxy with annual adjustments based on difference in maturity spreads between Tanzania and South Africa to consistently bring overall maturity spread estimates increasingly in line with evolving Tanzanian market fundamentals. Alternative proxies could have been derived from Kenya. An important consideration in determining a suitable proxy is the extent to which it is anticipated that the target market will develop along lines that parallel the benchmark market.

Based on an estimated benchmarked rate adjusted for maturity spread, a risk spread over the government bond rate must then be added to reflect commercial risk entailed in lending to mortgage financing entity. This risk spread should reflect actual rates used in other markets where there is some track record with mortgage financing institutions—at least until the target market has some hard domestic data on which to derive a locally based risk premium. This final price to the financial intermediary for on-lending to the PPP sponsor therefore comprises the following component parts:

Reference Rate + Maturity Spread + Risk Spread = Price to Financial Intermediary

What is important is the determination of the reference rate. That which is appropriate in Tanzania is not necessarily in other countries, particularly in West Africa, which has far fewer economic links to South Africa. In the case of the CFA zone countries and given the CFA link to the Euro, one possible benchmarking option for estimation of long-term CFA lending might be the Euro market in a similar the way that the Tanzania example used South African bond rates. Further analysis of prospective benchmarks for Ghana will be necessary to develop market-oriented long-term domestic pricing parameters to financial intermediaries. Another aspect of this effort to develop yield curve, which has been identified in Government of Ghana's Financial Sector Strategies, is to systematically issue longer-term bonds as a strategic approach to foster the establishment of longer-term prices.

To date, World Bank support to long-term local currency financing has adopted a variety of pricing approaches consistent with local market conditions, but has essentially followed the pricing strategy summarized above. Current Bank financing for longer-term infrastructure lending is summarized in table 6.1 below:

Table 6.1: World Bank Pricing Approaches to Long-Term Currency Financing

Country	Project	Financial Instrument	Intended Purpose	Tenor	Price and Product (variable/fixed spread)	Pricing against	Amount (US$ mn)
India	India Infrastructure Finance Company Limited (IIFCL)	Financial Intermediary Loan	Increase availability of long-term financing for infrastructure PPP	IIFCL Charter requires average maturity of 10 years. Lending has been for tenors of 13 up to 17 years in some cases.	IICL borrow from World Bank in US$ at LIBOR rate plus approx 50 bps for rupee-based on-lending. IICL on-lends rupees into market at commercial market rates currently in region of 10.5–12%. Depending on swap costs for US to Rupee, there is a mark-up for IIFCL of 75-100 bps. IIFCL can lend for up to two years beyond lead bank in consortium and is currently taking on more back-ended repayment structures. As IIFCL evolves its role in the market, it is developing new products including take-out financing arrangements to extend tenor offerings.	Market-rates with adjustments for swap costs of international funds.	1,195
Indonesia	Indonesia Infrastructure Finance Facility (IIFF)	Specific Investment Loan	Make available long-term infrastructure finance funds via local financial markets	N/A	Potential to develop a number of financial instruments based on following market price trends: Senior Loans: Loans of up to 15 years are expected to be a unique IIFF product. Bridge Finance: In Indonesia, this funding is available for a tenor of 3 months to 1 year with interest rates currently ranging from 15 to 20%. IIFF could potentially lengthen the maturity of these loans. Take-Out Finance and Refinance: Refinance can be provided to infrastructure providers or to commercial banks. Subordinated Debt: As a subordinated debt provider, the IIFF could provide first loss coverage to the commercial bankers, Securitization: The IIFF could contribute to the development of the market for securitized paper in the long run as regulatory constraints are addressed.	N/A	100
Nigeria	Public-Private Partnership Program (PPP)	Financial Intermediary Loan	Provide liquidity to the financial market to bring down cost of long-term debt finance	10-25 years	Currently estimated at 11.35, including a Forex and commercial risk mark-up to financial intermediary on moving average of 10 and 20 year government bond rates to be revised on constant basis	Average 10 and 20 year government bond rate	200

(Table continues on next page)

Table 6.1 (continued)

Country	Project	Financial Instrument	Intended Purpose	Tenor	Price and Product (variable/fixed spread)	Pricing against	Amount (US$ mn)
Bangladesh	Investment Promotion and Financing Facility (IPFF)	Financial Intermediary Loan	Provide long-term debt financing for PPPs	Up to 20 years but to date longest tenor has been 7 years	*Local currency loans :* Interest rate for a fixed rate bullet loan shall be set at 0.25 % above the equivalent maturity government bond rate. Interest rate for a fixed rate amortizing loan shall be set at 0.25% above the rate of the government bond having a maturity closest to the average life of the loan. The interest for a floating rate loan shall be set at 0.50 % above the interest rate of the Recipient's Treasury Bill maturing closest to the interest rest date of the loan. Interest rates for the government securities to be used as reference rates for Taka Facility Loans shall be as disclosed on the Bangladesh Bank's Web page	1-Year T-bill	297.5
West African Economic and Monetary Union (WAEMU)	WAEMU Capital Market Development Project	Financial Intermediary Loan	Provide long -term local infrastructure financing to WAEMU member countries	Up to 25 years with 7 - year grace	Initially 2% per annum on CFA funds to be reviewed annually. BOAD, the executing agent to carry Forex risk via an indexation clause to pass this risk to borrowers. These funds are lent to governments, not private sector.	Market-based	89.0
Peru	Guarantee Facility	Partial Risk Guarantee	Catalyze project finance against project risks	N/A	Cover up to 5 years government obligations over maximum of 15 years; local or USD- denominated debt	N/A	200

Note: Total amount reflects Bangladesh original project amount and additional financing.

The next key issue is the institutional arrangements for placing these funds effectively in the market. There are essentially three options. First, a Central Bank could, particularly where it has capacity and a track record in targeted lending activities, serve as the apex lender to financial intermediaries. This is the approach being taken by the Nigerian and Bangladeshi Governments. Funds would be on-lent to financial intermediaries looking to provide debt to PPP sponsors. This on-lending price would comprise the three component parts of benchmark and maturity and risk spread as set out above. These financial intermediaries would, in turn, need to show they have the project finance capacity and overall creditworthiness to effectively absorb long-term funds for which they would carry the commercial risk. A second route would be to assign this responsibility to a development bank in operation in the country. Given the recent track record of development banks, this option would require careful due diligence of the absorptive capacity of the selected development bank to undertake this responsibility. To avoid the large-scale failures of development banks in the 1970s and 1980s, Thorne and Toit (2009) identify six dimensions to be assessed in determining effectiveness and prospect of success for a development bank, namely: the enabling environment, mandate, regulation and supervision, governance and management, financial stability, and performance assessment. More specifically:

- *Their environment*: Development banks need a climate of macroeconomic stability without too many microeconomic distortions; they require political stability and a variety of complementary institutions. Although by definition their role is to address some of the weaknesses in the environment, they cannot succeed in a largely dysfunctional climate.
- *Their role*: They must be integrated into the financial system and operate along commercial lines, with a flexible mandate. They must not compete with the private sector, but rather aim to develop it. Once the private sector has the capacity to fund sectors previously funded by a development bank, the latter should be refocused on other areas of operation.
- *How they are controlled*: The ownership role of the state needs to be carried out circumspectly, allowing the bank to have operational autonomy while ensuring that it adheres to its mandate. The combined ownership and oversight role of government creates a potential conflict of interest that requires careful management. In general, the regulation and supervision of development banks should be along private sector lines.
- *How they are run*: Sound governance and management may be the single factor most likely to determine the success of a development bank. This involves issues such as the role and independence of the board; the accountability and capacity of management; the availability and retention of skilled staff; and sound operational, risk, and financial management.
- *How they are funded*: The government *needs to capitalize* new (or restructured) development banks adequately, and then limit additional fiscal support to ring-fenced noncommercial activities undertaken on behalf of the state. Development banks should be encouraged to approach donors and obtain a credit rating to enable them to raise funds on the capital markets.
- *Do they make a difference?* Development banks should be assessed on a regular basis against an agreed set of objectives, both financial and social or develop-

mental. Government must also be convinced that it could not have achieved these socially desirable outcomes in another (less expensive) way.

The third route is to set up a dedicated infrastructure financing entity. This entity could be wholly government owned (for example, the India Infrastructure Finance Company Ltd—IIFCL) or a public-private arrangement (for example, the Indonesia Infrastructure Finance Facility—IIFF), which can have an exit strategy for the government investment after the initial start-up period. There are different pros and cons to these two options. The IIFCL does not take a lead role in structuring PPP transactions. It is a lender that mostly comes in to assist financial parties close on PPP deals. The Indonesian IIFF—with its private sector shareholders and greater project finance expertise—has been designed to take more of a strategic project sponsorship role. Also, the government of Indonesia's thinking in establishing a private-public shareholding structure is to enhance its commercial credentials and attractiveness to future shareholders as well as provide a more ready exit strategy for the existing shareholders (government included, which will look to reduce overall shareholding as the IIFF establishes its track record). Both the IIFCL and the IIFF are authorized to raise funds locally, and IIFCL has the additional authority to raise funding internationally.

In deciding what institutional approach to take, a government also needs to determine what the timeframe is for getting this longer-term funding into the market and what sort of governance challenges it wants to take on. In particular, the establishment of a dedicated institution, with the legal and institutional considerations this entails (even if a clear view exists of whether this entity is to be public, private, or public-private in shareholding and governance) requires time. This can point to the need for a dual-track approach with a Central Bank or another established, suitably capacitated financial or development bank institution providing apex services until the new institution can become operational.

Risk Mitigation Guarantee Products

Embryonic PPP markets lacking track records in different sectors leave open a range of project risks that discourage private investment. These can comprise of a range of operational and market risks such as construction, demand, and foreign exchange risk, but most significant is often the government or political risk that PPP sponsors and financiers perceive. More specifically, the private investor wants to know whether a government will be able or willing to honor obligations under a PPP contract. This can encompass a Power Purchasing Agreement (PPA)\off-take agreements with an IPP; periodic tariff adjustments on power, road-toll, or water services; VGF and other types of payments (availability or annuity payments); or termination obligations. Different approaches to structuring guarantee services are relevant for these transactions. One option is to provide the guarantees on a case-by-case basis after due diligence is undertaken. The other option is to establish a guarantee fund that has a certain funding level to cover a number of PPP operations. The advantage of the first option is that it minimizes upfront exposure associated with a guarantee fund and also reduces the opportunity costs. This is particularly true when a country does not have a strong pipeline of projects likely to go promptly to market. Similarly, this is applicable where government policy and legislation are unclear, key government agencies appear not to be coordinated, and project development expertise is limited. Where this is the case, a fund-based government commitment to guarantee political risk could create significant moral hazard and associated contingent liability risks.

On the other hand, provided that the capacity exists to ensure that sound project development and enabling environment for PPPs is sufficiently well-established to attract credible investors, the establishment of a guarantee fund can provide an important signal to mobilize increased private sector interest and engagement. In the case of this approach, it is important —as reflected in the design of the Indonesia Infrastructure Guarantee Fund (IGF) to provide clear guidelines as to what risks are coverable through the fund. Such is the case in Brazil with the Partnership Guarantor Fund (PGF) deployed through the Banco do Brasil Distribuidora de titulos e Valores mobiliarios S.A.[6] In the Indonesia case, a number of different funding sources contribute to the IGF. Through its own capital, the IGF focuses on: (i) risks associated with government inaction or delay (allocation of land, issuance of permits and licenses); and (ii) weak creditworthiness of public sector contracting partners (particularly for off-take arrangements). Larger risks, where compensation is substantially in excess of the IGF capital base, such as can occur with termination risk or systemic breach of contract on financial obligations to PPP partner would be financed through the IGF from the Ministry of Finance. There are also efficiencies to be gained with the establishment of a fund in that it provides an institutional vehicle that can be supported by other investors. For instance, the World Bank is also contributing to the IGF through its PRG product, targeting a subset of project risks, including breach of contract, failure of government to honor scheduled tariff structures and adjustments as detailed in PPP contract, and changes in laws and regulations that adversely affect concessionaires' financial returns. Other guarantee-giving agencies could likewise be attracted to provide financing, subject to existence of viable project pipeline and sufficient PPP enabling environment. A government can then tailor different guarantee coverage across different financial sources in line with the risk coverage offered by the participating guarantee partners.

There is a range of guarantee products provided by different institutions. For instance, the World Bank and its sister agencies the Multilateral International Guarantee Agency (MIGA) and IFC- all provide guarantee instruments. The World Bank provides both Partial Credit Guarantees (PCG) and PRGs. The PCG seeks to provide credit risk coverage beyond maturities available from commercial lenders to extend tenors on private debt finance. The PRG offers partial mitigation against risk of default resulting from government nonperformance against a range of risks including: tariff, regulatory, collection, arbitration, changes in law, convertibility, transferability, and subsidy payments. In the case of MIGA, Box 6.1 below provides a summary of the political risks that it currently insures against. World Bank guarantees require a sovereign counter guarantee; the IFC and MIGA guarantee products do not, although the MIGA guarantees are only available when an international investor is part of the arrangement. The prices of these different guarantees vary based, inter alia, on the different conditions attached to them.

What is important to understand is that a risk guarantee fund is not a solution to lack of long-term liquidity. Its role is nevertheless critical, but is focused on specific project risks reflecting weaknesses—perceived and actual—in the enabling environment for PPPs. As this enabling environment—be it in the form of credit worthy off-takers, strengthened project development capacities, or improved intra-government coordina-

---

Box 6.1: Description of MIGA Coverage Products

TRANSFER RESTRICTION: Transfer Restriction Coverage protects against (i) the inability to convert from local currency into guarantee currency, loan payments, dividends, profits, and proceeds from the disposal of the guaranteed investment, and (ii) host government actions that prevent the transfer of the guarantee currency outside the host country, including the failure of the government to grant an authorization for the conversion or the transfer of such currency. Compensation is based on the guaranteed percentage of any payments that cannot be converted or transferred.

EXPROPRIATION: Expropriation Coverage protects against losses attributable to measures taken or approved by the host government that deprive the guarantee holder of its ownership or control over its investment, or in the case of debt, results in the project enterprise being unable to meet its obligations to the lender. Both direct and indirect (creeping) expropriation is covered. Compensation for equity is based on the guaranteed percentage of the net book value of the guaranteed investment in the project enterprise. For debt, compensation is based on the guaranteed percentage of the principal and interest that is in default as a result of expropriation.

WAR AND CIVIL DISTURBANCE: War and Civil Disturbance Coverage protects against losses arising as a result of military action or civil disturbance in the host country, including sabotage and terrorism, that destroys or damages tangible assets of the project enterprise or interferes with its operations (business interruption), or, in the case of debt, results in the project enterprise being unable to meet its obligations to the lender. Compensation is based on the guaranteed percentage of the value of the assets destroyed or damaged or, in the case of business interruption, the net book value of the guaranteed equity investment. For debt, compensation is based on the guaranteed percentage of the principal and interest that is in default as a result of war and civil disturbance.

BREACH OF CONTRACT: Breach of Contract Coverage protects against losses arising from a repudiation or breach by the host government of a contract entered with the guarantee holder, provided that a final and binding arbitration award or judicial decision has been rendered in favor of the guarantee holder and cannot be enforced against the host government. Compensation is based on the amount that the guarantee holder is entitled to recover from the host government in accordance with the terms of the arbitration award or judicial decision.

NON-HONORING OF SOVEREIGN FINANCIAL OBLIGATION: Non-Honoring of Sovereign Financial Obligation Coverage protects against losses resulting from a government's failure to make a payment when due under an unconditional financial payment obligation or guarantee given in favor of a project that otherwise meets all of MIGA's normal requirements. It does not require the investor to obtain an arbitral award. This coverage is applicable in situations when a sovereign's financial payment obligation is unconditional and not subject to defenses.

---

tion or sector policies—becomes more robust and track records are established, the need for substantial guarantee arrangements will diminish. In the interim, guarantees can prove critical to the flow of equity and debt financing.

PPP Market Failures Deriving from Country Size and Cross-Border Infrastructure Financing Constraints

Two strong PPP market failures requiring more regional solutions are widely apparent in Africa. First, economically smaller nations that are often landlocked or have other intrinsic growth-inhibiting characteristics fail to attract quality private sector investors. As seen in the earlier part of this paper, this is the result of the thinness of their capital markets and inability to compete with their more commercially visible neighbors. Secondly, cross-border infrastructure deficits retard trade by driving up the cost of moving goods and providing regional services. Poor core infrastructure limits trade and prevents both small and large firms from conducting business and expanding their services. Tackling these two market failures to PPP financing for small landlocked countries and cross-border infrastructure requires a regional financing approach. More specifically, the continent's RECs, such as ECOWAS, SADC, and EAC can play key roles in supporting public-private partnership investment in infrastructure.

Recent Bank experience working at the regional level in Africa to support infrastructure financing has been limited and mixed. A 2004 Capital Market Development project executed by the Banque Ouest-Africaine de Développement (BOAD) to provide long-term 25-year financing for infrastructure projects had limited initial success largely because of procurement capacity limitations with member governments and the BOAD.[7] This experience, however, does highlight two significant positives outcomes. First, it has shown the important role that a regional institution can play in addressing infrastructure financing gaps in smaller countries. It also points to the comparative advantage of locating key project development (including procurement) expertise in a regional institution in order to achieve some scale economies in the utilization of expensive project development and finance expertise. Identifying suitable institutions to take on these regional dimensions of PPP markets will be critical. Regional institutions with particular financing mandates, such as the BOAD, can take a lead in the financing of PPPs and PPP project development as well. It could also involve other existing financial institutions with regional coverage. This may include quasi-public entities such as the African Finance Corporation as well as commercial banks with a continent-wide or sub-regional presence. Finally, the institutions of the existing RECs are also potential sources for PPP expertise, particularly in project development. This is relevant for countries for which the domestic PPP market is too small to merit investing in its own PPP Resource Centre.

Notes

1. See section 5.1 of the Government of India's "Scheme and Guidelines for Financial Support to Public Private Partnerships in Infrastructure," 2008, from www.pppinindia.com.
2. See Annex 1, Section 4, Paragraph 2 of the government of India "Scheme and Guidelines for Financial Support to Public Private Partnerships in Infrastructure," 2008, from www.pppinindia.com.
3. World Bank (2009), p. 38.
4. See Annex 9, World Bank Project Appraisal Document, Report number 52750-TZ, February 10th 2010 for Housing Finance Project.
5. Abbas, S.M. A. and Yuri Sobolev (2008).
6. Arrobas, Daniele La Porta and Jose Virgilia Lopes Enei (January 2009).
7. Reference WAEMU Capital Market Development Project, Project Appraisal Document, Report No: 27518-AFR, January 28, 2004.

CHAPTER 7

Recommendations

The primary focus of this report is to preliminarily scope out and describe the factors affecting long-term financing for PPPs in the sample countries, as well as describe current PPP initiatives highlighting the general challenges regarding the enabling environment. In this respect, the policy recommendations outlined in this section address the most pressing challenges that have been outlined in this study, and are deliberately broad in nature. The discussed suggestions are meant to lay the groundwork for more in-depth country-specific and technical analysis that will explore and expand upon the concepts touched upon.

Developing Long-Term Financing for Infrastructure

Governments can support structural reforms to enhance local sources of infrastructure financing by developing the local capital market. This includes the government and nongovernment bond markets, the equity market, and pension and insurance funds. Developing a liquid domestic government bond market with a long-term yield curve is a critical first step needed to provide a benchmark that is fundamental for the pricing of credit risk associated with long-term financing. Policy reforms geared toward developing the local capital market are also critical. For instance, building up a debt market for nongovernment bonds offers the ideal mechanism by which pension funds and insurance companies can directly invest in infrastructure projects. Additionally, increasing the capacity of the local stock market to absorb a large public offering of shares would significantly increase available long-term financing operation for the development of physical infrastructure. Achieving an acceptable level of capital market development and ensuring transparency and sound governance can trigger revising investment regulations pertaining to pension and insurance funds to accommodate infrastructure financing.

Until such long tenor markets are developed, governments can provide private projects sponsors with long-term finance through commercially based on-lending. Developing a sound long-term financing system for local currency is a medium- to long-term effort. Until such markets progress, the government can facilitate access to long-term local currency debt by funding prequalified local financial intermediaries for subsequent on-lending to project sponsors. Governments can obtain support from IFIs to establish such facilities. In countries like Mexico (Banobras) and Brazil (BNDSE), the government has been channeling significant amounts of financing to the infrastructure sector through their specialized development banks, which either gets funding from the local and international capital markets or from IFIs. Such institutions have lent the funds directly to the projects or they use commercial banks to deploy the funds. These institutions have also acted as credit enhancers to help projects raise less expensive long-term money.

The public sector should provide tools that enhance private sector engagement such as risk mitigation products and financial incentives. Government must be ready to take on some risks that may traditionally be captured by the private sector. There are a number of risk mitigation products, financial incentives, and other tools that would serve to address constraints and enhance financial sector engagement in infrastructure financing. These include:

- *Supporting PPP projects with a VGF to reduce the entrance cost for the private sector and make infrastructure assets more commercially viable.* The VGF is a facility that provides a mechanism to channel public capital to plug funding gaps required to make infrastructure PPP projects bankable and commercially viable. These funds can be used for projects with great upfront capital requirements where an initial contribution from the government, or payments over time, may be required to make the project financially viable, thus attracting the interest of private sector investors. The facility can also be used to induce the commercial viability of projects with very high levels of uncertainty on demand or user affordability constraints, but for which there is still a powerful justification for private sector involvement and management.
- *Developing intermediate pricing strategies that contribute to the lengthening of the yield curve in ways that build the long-term debt market.* This can include strategic longer-term bond issues and the type of price building that is being pursued in the Tanzania mortgage market.
- *Providing mitigation products for political risk.* Political risk embedded in the government's failure to comply with its explicit contractual obligations to its private sector partner is one of the most important considerations for both debt and equity providers. Examples of instruments that can be used to reduce this risk include MIGA risk mitigation products such as breach of contract and non-honoring of sovereign financial obligation, and the IBRD/IDA PRG guarantee. Notably the latter could also be used to guarantee public sector contributions to projects through the VGF.
- *Developing PPP roles for RECs and regionally active financial institutions.* This will address the additional market failures that can impact smaller economies and address regional infrastructure needs.

Strengthening Other Aspects of a Strong Enabling Environment

Build a clear and transparent PPP institutional framework. The private sector responds favorably to simple, clear, and transparent institutional arrangements with easily followed procedures for how to engage the public sector. A sound institutional framework also signals a government's long-term commitment to its PPP program to the market as well as institutionalizing best practices and procedures for all MDAs to utilize. Standardizing PPP project development and monitoring eliminates many opportunities for political interests to interfere with the transaction. When setting up the institutional framework, attention must be made to address the many sides of PPP transactions from project development to contract compliance. Institutional framework solutions for each country will vary undoubtedly, but the shared principles upon which all are built should adhere to international best practices, incorporate lessons learned, and target simplicity, efficiency, and transparency. Furthermore PPP projects involve a number of players, namely: the ministry of finance, line MDAs, investors, financiers, and private concessionaires. A well-established institutional and operational framework ensures that responsibilities and decision rights are rationally allocated to the appropriate public and private parties, with conflicts of interest avoided.

Solidify a robust PPP enabling legal and regulatory environment. This can be achieved by drawing on international best practices in drafting of PPP laws, policies, regulations, and guidelines. Diligence should be given to ensuring that these primary and secondary legislations (including tariff policies that need to be reformed to accommodate cost-recovery mechanisms) are harmonized with existing procurement, financial management, and sector policies. For example, one danger frequently encountered is drafting of a PPP law before solidifying a PPP policy first. As a result, arrangements that are not sustainable or not best practice become entrenched in law and are thereafter difficult to amend. The creation first of a PPP policy provides an excellent forum for the public sector to build policy consensus, increase understanding of PPPs across MDAs, and identify further weaknesses at the sector level. Experience has shown that upstream diagnostic studies to assist governments to address these challenges have been a useful and prudent approach to building a sound PPP program. In general, a well-defined PPP legislation in the public domain binds governments by general principles of good governance.

Building capacity of MDAs is critical to the success of a PPP program. Capacity building programs are important for establishing a common base of PPP knowledge and best practices across key MDAs. This includes MDAs leading PPP transactions in each sector as well as other MDAs playing supporting roles in the project development cycle such as procurement (bidding processes), financial management, and compliance. The comprehensive characteristics of PPPs make it essential that all government entities involved in the PPP process be equipped to understand, identify, and evaluate PPP projects, in addition to being trained to the particularities of interactions with the multiple private parties involved (transaction advisor, concessionaire, financier, and investors). Capacity building programs that range from general PPP awareness to technically specific topics and sector-specific topics should be provided to all key stakeholders involved in the PPP program.

Governments need to communicate effectively the rationale and benefits of PPPs to ensure public support. Even technically sound PPP projects can fail without a full understanding of the surrounding sociopolitical dynamics. Public asset divestment programs undertaken by governments tend to be under severe scrutiny from civil society organizations and citizens. It is thus crucial to incorporate communication analysis and stakeholder engagement at the policy and program formulation stage.

Provide budgetary support for producing a quality pipeline of PPP projects that employs upstream feasibility analysis to review projects properly and outline any government contributions deemed necessary to make the project commercially viable. Deal flows of viable bankable projects are the prime constraint that the private sector faces as it embarks on investing in PPPs. The process of reviewing the projects upstream will assist in thinking through project-specific issues at an early stage. A feasibility study verifies whether the proposed project is well founded and is likely to meet the needs of its intended target groups and beneficiaries. In addition, the study defines the operational details of the project, taking account of all policy, technical, economic, financial, institutional, management, environmental, socio-cultural, and gender-related aspects, thereby providing government with sufficient information to justify acceptance, modification, or rejection of the proposed project. It is during the project appraisal process that the government determines whether or not to proceed with a PPP. More specifically, the feasibility study confirms three criteria on which PPP projects are based: affordability, VfM, and risk. As noted in the report, the cost of such studies may be significant and can reach up to 10 percent of the project value. Budgetary support to line ministries to enable undertaking such rigorous and essential analysis should be considered.[1]

Initiate the PPP program with pilot demonstration projects to showcase a successful transaction. It is crucial that the first PPPs going to the market are successful. The first several PPP transactions will have particularly high visibility among international stakeholders. If these deals are well structured and are professionally developed, they could attract enormous attention from world-class advisors, investors, financiers, and other private sector participants for the pipeline of transactions to follow. If, on the other hand, the first projects are not successfully executed, it could tarnish the program's reputation and represent a serious obstacle to the program moving forward on a meaningful scale. Additionally, well-executed first-mover projects will have the virtue of creating a valuable demonstration effect domestically. This illustrates to MDAs the value of rigorous project preparation, assessment, and transparent and competitive market procurement. The size of the transaction is an important criterion for first-mover projects; they should be large enough to attract a broad range of bidders, including international proponents, but at the same time not so large as to pose a bottleneck, particularly in financing. Furthermore, project-specific factors can have a far greater impact on risk and therefore suitability for first-mover transactions than sector considerations. For example, it is not inconceivable that a large Greenfield road project might be less appropriate as a first-mover transaction than an operating agreement for a major existing airport with high-quality historical enplanement data.

Sponsoring governments should not underestimate the role of the effective management of fiscal liabilities related to PPPs and should develop their administrative capacity to undertake such task. Critical to successful management of PPPs is understanding that implementing PPPs does not mean a free provision of infrastructure. While the PPP financial model caters to current infrastructure deficits, it mortgages governments' future revenue. PPP fiscal commitments, which take the form of government debt or revenue guarantees offered to a service provider to make a project seem less risky and more attractive to the private investors, create fiscal risks and uncertainties for governments and can ultimately increase their debt burdens. Governments should get their incentives right by not adopting PPPs to get around debt constraints and accounting rules, but rather for the expected efficiency gains.

Finally, it is important to manage government expectations regarding what one can expect from private participation in infrastructure, with respect to the size of their contribution and also the time required for processing PPP projects. While the private sector can significantly contribute to public services provision, the bulk of infrastructure will remain a government responsibility. It is worthwhile to note that PPP projects in the UK under the Private Finance Initiative (PFI) make up 10-15 percent of public's sector investment, and account for 20 percent and 15 percent of Spain's and Korea's infrastructure investment, respectively. This indicates a benchmark in countries where PPPs have been active for at least a decade. Additionally and in light of the complexity of designing PPPs, they require lead time which can be longer that those needed under public procurement. For instance in the UK average time needed to reach financial close has varied from 18 months for the roads sector to 40 months for the health sector[2].

Notes

1. IP3: www.ip3.org.
2. EIB (2010).

References

Abbas, S.M.A., and Yuri Sobodly (2008). "High and Volatile Yields in Tanzania: The Role of Strategic Bidding and Auction Microstructure." IMF, Washington, DC.

ABSA Capital (2010). "Africa Local Markets Guide: A Focus on SSA Markets."

African Securities Exchange Association (ASES). Year Book 2009.

Andres, Luis (2004). "The Impact of Privatization on Firms in the Infrastructure Sector in Latin American Countries," PhD Dissertation, University of Chicago.

Andres, Luis, V. Foster, and L. Guasch (2006). "The Impact of Privatization on the Performance of Infrastructure Sector: The Case of Electricity Distribution in Latin American Countries." Policy Research Working Paper 3936. World Bank, Washington, DC.

Arrobas, Daniele La Porta and Jose Virgilia Lopes Enei. (January 2009) "Brazil: Framework Analysis for Public-Private Partnerships in Irrigation." World Bank and PPIAF. Washington, DC.

Asia-Pacific Economic Cooperation Presentation in Japan (June 2010). "Private Financing of Infrastructure in Asia." Asian Development Bank.

Banco Bilbao Vizcaya Argentaria-BBVA (2010). "A Balance and Projections of the Experience in Infrastructure of Pension Funds in Latin America."

Bullock, R (2005). "Results of Railway Privatization in Africa." Unpublished manuscript. World Bank, Washington, DC.

Bullock, R (2009). "Africa Infrastructure Country Diagnostic: Railways in Sub-Saharan Africa." Unpublished manuscript. World Bank, Washington, DC.

Briceño-Garmendia, Cecilia, Karlis Smits, and Vivien Foster (2008). "Financing Public Infrastructure in Sub-Saharan Africa: Patterns, Issues, and Options." Background Paper 15, Africa Infrastructure Country Diagnostic. World Bank, Washington, DC.

Cochran, T. (2009). "Financial Institutions Appetite for Nigerian Core Infrastructure Financing in the Wake of the Global Financial Crisis: The Short, Medium and Long Term." Unpublished manuscript. World Bank and PPIAF, Washington, DC.

Di Borgo, P. (2006). "Review of Selected Railway Concessions in Sub-Saharan Africa." Unpublished manuscript. World Bank, Washington, DC.

Dos Santos Senna, L.A., and Michael F. Dutra (2008). *Rodovias Auto-sustentadas: Desafio do Seculo XXI*, Editora CLA Cultural Ltda., São Paulo, Brazil.

Efficient Securities Markets Institutional Development- ESMID (2010) "Total Outstanding Corporate and Sub-National Bonds Issued 2009 to September 30th." Unpublished Manuscript. World Bank, Washington, DC.

Engel, E. (2010) Presentation "Public Private Partnerships: When and How." ICIED. Toulouse.

European Investment Bank- EIB (2010). "Public and Private Financing of Infrastructure: Evolution and Economics of Private Infrastructure Finance."

Foster, V., W. Butterfield, C. Chen, and N. Pushak (2008). "Building Bridges: China's Growing Role as Infrastructure Financier for Sub-Saharan Africa." World Bank-PPIAF, Washington, DC.

Foster, Vivien, and Cecilia Briceño-Garmendia, eds. (2010). "Africa's Infrastructure: A Time for Transformation." World Bank, Washington, DC.

Fédération des Sociétés d'assurances De Droit National Africaines - FANAF (2010). "Annuaire des Sociétés membres de la FANAF," Dadar, Senegal.

Gassner, K., A. Popov and N. Pushak (2008). "Does Private Sector Participation Improve Performance in Electricity and Water Distribution?" World Bank-PPIAF, Washington, DC.

Guasch, J. L. (2004). "Granting and Renegotiating Infrastructure Concession: Doing it Right." The World Bank, Washington, DC.

Hahm, J. (2010). WBI presentation, "Institutional Framework for PPPs." World Bank, Washington, DC.

Inderst, G. (2009). "Pension Fund Investment in Infrastructure." OECD Working Papers on Insurance and Private Pensions, No. 32. OECD publishing, Paris.

IMF (April 2010). "Regional Economic Outlook-Sub Saharan Africa (SSA)." Washington, DC.

IMF (October 2010). "Regional Economic Outlook-Sub Saharan Africa (SSA)." Washington, DC.

Infrastructure Investor website (January 2010). "Britain's PPP Bashing."

Irving, J. and A. Manroth (2009). "Local Sources of Financial for Infrastructure in Africa: A Cross Country Analysis." World Bank, Washington, DC.

Irwin, T. and Tanya Mokdad (2009). "Managing contingent liabilities in public-private partnerships: Practice in Australia, Chile, and South Africa."

Kim, J. (2008) "Fiscal Risk Management in PPPs." Presentation in the 3rd Annual Meeting on PPP Promotion between Japan and Korea.

Matsukawa, Tomoko, R. Sheppard, and J Wright (2003). "Foreign Exchange Rate Mitigation for Power and Water Projects in Developing Countries." World Bank, Washington, DC.

New Partnership for Africa's Development—Organization for Economic Co-operation and Development (NEPAD-OECD) (2008). "Emerging Public and Sovereign Fund Investors in Africa's Infrastructure Challenges and Perspectives."

Organization for Economic Co-operation and Development (OECD) (2007). "Infrastructure to 2030: Main Findings and Policy Recommendations."

OECD/IOPS Meeting in Kenya (2008). "Infrastructure Investment and Pension funds in Latin America." Kenya.

OECD (2007). Infrastructure to 2030: Main Findings and Policy Recommendations.

Private Participation in Infrastructure (PPI) Database. http://ppi.worldbank.org/.

PPIAF Gridline Notes (2006). "Financing Infrastructure in Africa: How the Region Can Attract More Project Finance."

PPIAF Gridlines (2007a). "Designing and using PPP units in infrastructure: Lessons from case studies around the world."

PPIAF Gridline Notes (2007b). "Unsolicited Infrastructure Proposals: How some countries introduce competition and transparency."

Retirement Benefit Authority (RBA) presentation (January 2007). "The Kenya and Pension Fund Market."

Robertson, D. (2008). "Dubai International Capital Looks East as It Confirms Plans to Retreat from Western Markets." London, *Times of London*.

Sein, P. (2006). "Evaluation of PPPs—Preliminary Assessment." Presentation at OECD Symposium on Private Partnerships. Madrid, July 5-7.

Thorne and Toit (2009). "A macro-framework for successful development banks." *Development Southern Africa* 26(5).

World Bank. (2009). "Infrastructure Funds and Facilities in Sub-Saharan Africa." Unpublished manuscript. World Bank, Washington, DC.

World Bank (2010). "Kenya: Nongovernment Bond Market Development Technical Note." Unpublished manuscript. World Bank, Washington, DC.

World Bank & PPIAF. (2009). "Financial Institutions Appetite for Nigerian Core Infrastructure Financing in the Wake of the Global Financial Crisis: The Short, Medium and Long Term." Unpublished manuscript. World Bank, Washington, DC.

World Bank & Axelcium (2010). "Analysis of the Financial Crisis Impact Upon Infrastructure Financing Capabilities of Ivory Coast, Senegal and Cameroon." Unpublished manuscript. World Bank, Washington, DC.

World Bank & Castalia (2010). "Support for the Implementation of Fiscal Commitment and Contingent Liability Management Framework for PPPs in Nigeria." Unpublished manuscript. World Bank, Washington DC.

World Bank & IP3 (2007). "Consultancy Services for the Consolidation, Strengthening and Harmonization of Policy, Legal and institutional Framework for Public Private Partnership (PPP)." Unpublished manuscript. World Bank, Washington DC.

Yescombe, R. (2007). *Public Private Partnerships: Principles of Policy and Finance*. Oxford, UK: Elsevier.

ECO-AUDIT
Environmental Benefits Statement

The World Bank is committed to preserving endangered forests and natural resources. The Office of the Publisher has chosen to print World Bank Studies and Working Papers on recycled paper with 30 percent postconsumer fiber in accordance with the recommended standards for paper usage set by the Green Press Initiative, a non-profit program supporting publishers in using fiber that is not sourced from endangered forests. For more information, visit www.greenpressinitiative.org.

In 2010, the printing of this book on recycled paper saved the following:
- 11 trees*
- 3 million Btu of total energy
- 1,045 lb. of net greenhouse gases
- 5,035 gal. of waste water
- 306 lb. of solid waste

*40 feet in height and 6–8 inches in diameter

CPSIA information can be obtained at www.ICGtesting.com
Printed in the USA
269872BV00004B/1/P